MW01243151

TRUE STORIES OF NEBRASKA PIONEERS

{ILLUSTRATED AND ANNOTATED}

Selections from:

COLLECTION OF
NEBRASKA PIONEER
REMINISCENCES

ISSUED BY THE

**NEBRASKA SOCIETY OF
THE DAUGHTERS OF THE
AMERICAN REVOLUTION**

NINETEEN SIXTEEN

THE TORCH PRESS

CEDAR RAPIDS

IOWA

Published by Knowledge Keepers, U.S. A.

2020

ISBN: 9798569194018

Cover design:

Nicki Truesdell

TABLE OF CONTENTS

Publisher's Note   i

Forethought   iii

Map, Nebraska 1914   v

EARLY DAYS IN FREMONT
BY MRS. THERON NYE   1

RECOLLECTIONS OF THE FIRST SETTLER OF
DAWSON COUNTY
BY MRS. DANIEL FREEMAN   9

PIONEER JUSTICE
BY B. F. KRIER   13

EARLY EXPERIENCES IN ADAMS COUNTY
BY GENERAL ALBERT V. COLE   16

A BROKEN AXLE
BY SAMUEL C. BASSETT   22

EXPERIENCES OF A PIONEER WOMAN
BY MRS. ELISE G. EVERETT   26

RECOLLECTIONS OF WEEPING WATER,
NEBRASKA
BY I. N. HUNTER   30

INCIDENTS AT PLATTSMOUTH
BY ELLA POLLOCK MINOR   34

REMINISCENCES OF CUSTER COUNTY
BY MRS. J. J. DOUGLAS   36

LIFE ON THE FRONTIER
BY JAMES AYRES   41

EARLY RECOLLECTIONS
BY C. CHABOT   45

EARLY DAYS IN DAWSON COUNTY
BY LUCY R. HEWITT   48

A GRASSHOPPER STORY
BY MARGARET F. KELLY   54

PIONEERING IN FILLMORE COUNTY
BY JOHN R. MCCASHLAND   56

REMINISCENCES OF GAGE COUNTY
BY ALBERT L. GREEN   59

RANCHING IN GAGE AND JEFFERSON
COUNTIES
BY PETER JANSEN   72

EARLY RECOLLECTIONS OF GAGE COUNTY
BY MRS. E. JOHNSON   78

A BUFFALO HUNT
BY W. H. AVERY   81

A GRASSHOPPER RAID
BY EDNA M. BOYLE ALLEN   83

EARLY DAYS IN PAWNEE COUNTY
BY DANIEL B. CROPSEY   86

THE EARLIEST ROMANCE OF JEFFERSON
COUNTY, NEBRASKA
BY GEORGE W. HANSEN   90

EXPERIENCES ON THE FRONTIER
BY FRANK HELVEY   95

LOOKING BACKWARD
BY GEORGE E. JENKINS   99

THE EASTER STORM OF 1873
BY CHARLES B. LETTON   102

EARLY EXPERIENCES IN NEBRASKA
BY ELIZABETH PORTER SEYMOUR   106

LINCOLN IN THE EARLY SEVENTIES
BY (MRS. O. C.) MINNIE DEETTE POLLEY BELL   110

GRAY EAGLE, PAWNEE CHIEF
BY MILLARD S. BINNEY   113

EARLY INDIAN HISTORY
BY MRS. SARAH CLAPP   116

THE BLIZZARD OF 1888
BY MINNIE FREEMAN PENNEY   123

MY TRIP WEST IN 1861
BY SARAH SCHOOLEY RANDALL   127

STIRRING EVENTS ALONG THE LITTLE BLUE
BY CLARENDON E. ADAMS   131

MY LAST BUFFALO HUNT
BY J. STERLING MORTON   138

HOW THE FOUNDER OF ARBOR DAY CREATED
THE MOST FAMOUS WESTERN ESTATE
BY PAUL MORTON   157

EARLY REMINISCENCES OF NEBRASKA CITY
By ELLEN KINNEY WARE 163

SOME PERSONAL INCIDENTS
By W. A. MCALLISTER 166

MAJOR NORTH'S BUFFALO HUNT
By MINNIE FREEMAN PENNY 168

PIONEER LIFE
By MRS. JAMES G. REEDER 170

EARLY DAYS IN POLK COUNTY
By CALMAR MCCUNE 174

PERSONAL REMINISCENCES
By MRS. THYRZA REAVIS ROY 179

SEWARD COUNTY REMINISCENCES
COMPILED BY MARGARET HOLMES CHAPTER D. A. R.
182

PIONEERING
By GRANT LEE SHUMWAY 191

EARLY DAYS IN STANTON COUNTY
Statement by Andrew J. Bottorff 195

FRED E. ROPER, PIONEER
By ERNEST E. CORRELL 198

AN INDIAN RAID
BY ERNEST E. CORRELL 202

REMINISCENCES
By MRS. E. A. RUSSELL 205

REMINISCENCES OF FORT CALHOUN
BY W. H. ALLEN   208

REMINISCENCES OF WASHINGTON COUNTY
BY MRS. EMILY BOTTORFF ALLEN   211

REMINISCENCES OF DE SOTO IN 1855
BY OLIVER BOUVIER   214

THE STORY OF THE TOWN OF FONTENELLE
BY MRS. EDA MEAD   216

THE LAST ROMANTIC BUFFALO HUNT ON THE
PLAINS OF NEBRASKA
BY JOHN LEE WEBSTER   223

PUBLISHER'S NOTE

The American pioneers are a fascinating group of people. Average men and women, often with a string of children in tow, would sell all that they owned, move into a covered wagon, and set out for a wilderness they had never seen. Knowing that there would be no friends to welcome them, no comfortable house to rent, and no store to purchase supplies from, they eagerly anticipated a land where there was at least a chance to build and dream.

The journey westward was tough enough, with river crossings, sickness, wagon repairs, and even death, but their new lives would involve even more. Indian attacks, grasshopper plagues, blizzards, drought--- it would be enough to drive a 21st century American to tears.

And while some did experience grief and frustration, and a few gave up and went back East, the majority stayed on in the new lands of the West. They blazed ahead with what little they had, formed community, created towns, founded churches and schools, and helped to build a nation.

We owe so much to those brave men and women. I am thankful for their grit, their faith, and for their foresight to share a bit of their stories. I am also thankful to organizations like Daughters of the American Revolution for compiling and preserving this history. This is what Knowledge Keepers strives to share.

I have not altered the original text in any way. However, I have added photographs of the storytellers and a bit of their biographies whenever possible, and in some cases I updated punctuation and paragraph spacing for ease of reading. I hope you will enjoy this unique bit of American history and pass it on to your children and grandchildren.

Nicki Truesdell

Founder, Knowledge Keepers

September 2020

FORETHOUGHT

This Book of Nebraska Pioneer Reminiscences is issued by the Daughters of the American Revolution of Nebraska, and dedicated to the daring, courageous, and intrepid men and women—the advance guard of our progress—who, carrying the torch of civilization, had a vision of the possibilities which now have become realities.

To those who answered the call of the unknown we owe the duty of preserving the record of their adventures upon the vast prairies of "Nebraska the Mother of States."

"In her horizons, limitless and vast
Her plains that storm the senses like the sea."

Reminiscence, recollection, personal experience—simple, true stories—this is the foundation of History.

Rapidly the pioneer story-tellers are passing beyond recall, and the real story of the beginning of our great commonwealth must be told now.

The memories of those pioneers, of their deeds of self-sacrifice and devotion, of their ideals which are our inheritance, will inculcate patriotism in the children of the future; for they should realize the courage that subdued the wilderness. And "lest we forget," the heritage of this past is a sacred trust to the Daughters of the American Revolution of Nebraska.

The invaluable assistance of the Nebraska State Historical Society, and the members of this Book Committee, Mrs. C. S. Paine, and Mrs. D. S. Dalby, is most gratefully acknowledged.

LULA CORRELL PERRY
(Mrs. Warren Perry)

1915

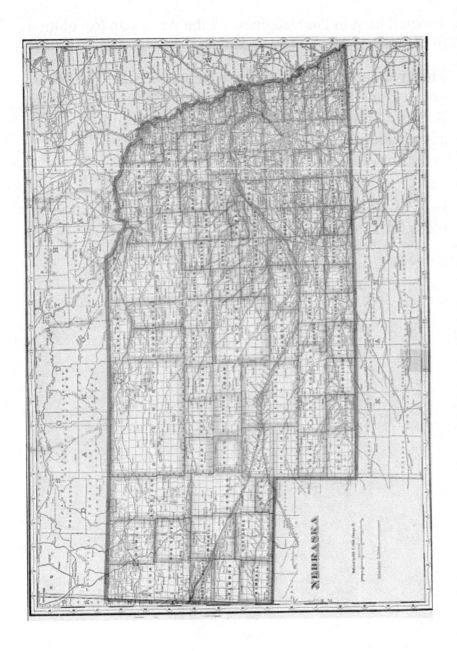

NEBRASKA

EARLY DAYS IN FREMONT

BY MRS. THERON NYE

From the year 1856 until the beginning of the civil war in 1861 the early settlers of Nebraska experienced nearly all of the ills and hardships incidental to a pioneer life. Fifty years have passed since then and to one having lived through those trying days—or to a stranger who merely listens to the almost incredulous tales of a past generation—there arises a question as to why any sane person or persons should desire to leave a land of comparative comfort and plenty for one of deprivation and possible starvation.

The early settlers of Fremont were, for the most part. young people from the eastern states, full of ambition and hope. There is, in the youthful heart, a spirit of energy, of doing and daring in order to realize, if possible, dreams of a perhaps glorious future in which may be won honor and fame and wealth. Then again, the forces of nature are never at rest and man, being a part of the great whole, must inevitably keep in step with the universal law. A few lines written for a paper several years ago give the first impression of the landscape which greeted the eyes of a stranger on entering the valley of the Elkhorn river in 1858, April 26:

"This is the picture as I see it plainly in retrospect—a country, and it was all a country, with a smooth, level, gray surface which appeared to go on toward the west forever and forever. On the north were the bluffs of the Elkhorn river, but the great Elkhorn Valley was a part of an unknown world. South of the little townsite of Fremont the Platte river moved sluggishly along to meet and be swallowed up in the great Missouri. Ten or twelve log cabins broke the monotony of the treeless expanse that stretched far away, apparently to a leaden sky. My heart sank within me as I thought but did not say, 'How can I ever live in a place like this?'" And yet the writer of the above lines has lived in Fremont for forty-seven years.

The histories of the world are chiefly men's histories. They are stories of governments, of religions, of wars, and only in exceptional instances has woman appeared to hold any important place in the affairs of nations. From the earliest settlement of the colonies in the new world until the present time, women have not only borne with bravery and fortitude the greater trials of the pioneer life, but from their peculiar organization and temperament suffered more from the small annoyances than their stronger companions of the other sex. The experiences of the home and family life of the early settlers of the great West have never entered into the annals of history nor can a truthful story be told without them, but thus far no doubt the apparent neglect has been due to woman herself, who until quite recently has felt that she was a small factor in the world's affairs.

In the beginning of the new life in Fremont women had their first introduction to the log cabin which was to be their home for many years. It was not as comfortable as it looks picturesque and romantic printed on paper. It was a story and a half high, sixteen by twenty feet in size. The logs were hewn on two sides, but the work performed by the volunteer carpenters of that time was not altogether satisfactory, consequently the logs did not fit closely but the open spaces between were filled with a sort of mortar that had a faculty of gradually dropping off as it dried, leaving the original holes and openings through which the winter winds whistled and Nebraska breezes blew the dirt.

The houses were made of cottonwood logs and finished with cottonwood lumber. The shingles warped so the roof somewhat resembled a sieve. The rain dripped through it in summer and snow sifted through it in winter. The floors were made of wide rough boards, the planing and polishing given by the broom, the old-fashioned mop, and the scrubbing brush. The boards warped and shrunk so that the edges turned up, making wide cracks in the floor through which many small articles dropped down into a large hole in the ground miscalled a cellar. It was hardly possible to keep from freezing in these houses in winter. Snow sifted through the roof, covering beds and floors. The piercing winds blew through every crack and crevice. Green cottonwood was the only fuel obtainable and that would sizzle and fry in the stove while water froze standing under the stove. This is no fairy tale.

The summers were not much more pleasant. It must be remembered that there were no trees in Fremont, nothing that afforded the least protection from the hot rays of a Nebraska sun. Mosquitoes and flies were in abundance, and door screens were unknown at that time. The cotton netting nailed over windows and hung over and around the beds was a slight protection from the pests, although as the doors must necessarily be opened more or less no remedy could be devised that would make any perceptible improvement. To submit was the rule and the law in those days, but many, many times it was done under protest.

The first floor was divided or partitioned off, by the use of quilts or blankets, into a kitchen, bedroom, and pantry. The chamber, or what might be called attic, was also partitioned in the same way, giving as many rooms as it would hold beds. The main articles of food for the first two years consisted of potatoes, corn meal, and bacon. The meal was made from a variety of corn raised by the Indians and called Pawnee corn. It was very soft, white, and palatable. Wheat flour was not very plentiful the first year. Bacon was the only available meat. Occasionally a piece of buffalo meat

3

was obtained, but it being very hard to masticate only served to make a slight change in the gravy, which was otherwise made with lard and flour browned together in an iron frying pan, adding boiling water until it was of the right consistency, salt and pepper to suit the taste. This mixture was used for potatoes and bread of all kinds. Lard was a necessity. Biscuits were made of flour, using a little corn meal for shortening and saleratus for raising. Much of the corn was ground in an ordinary coffee mill or in some instances rubbed on a large grater or over a tin pan with a perforated bottom, made so by driving nails through it. The nearest flouring mill was at Fort Calhoun, over forty miles away, which was then a three days' journey, taking more time than a trip to California at the present day. Nothing, however, could be substituted for butter. The lack of meat, sugar, eggs and fruit, tea and coffee, was borne patiently, but wheat flour and corn meal bread with its everlasting lard gravy accompaniment was more than human nature could bear, yet most of the people waxed strong and flourished on bread and grease. Oh, where are the students of scientific research and domestic economy? There were possibly three or four cows in the settlement, and if there was ever an aristocracy in Fremont, it was represented by the owners of said cows.

In 1858 a little sorghum was raised. "Hope springs eternal in the human breast." Men, women, and children helped to prepare the stalks when at the right stage for crushing, which was done with a very primitive home-made machine. The juice obtained was boiled down to syrup, but alas, the dreams of a surfeit of sweetness vanished into thin air, for the result of all the toil and trouble expended was a production so nauseous that it could not be used even for vinegar.

Wild plums and grapes grew in profusion on the banks of the rivers. There was much more enjoyment in gathering the fruit than in eating or cooking it. The plums were bitter and sour, the grapes were sour and mostly seeds, and sugar was not plentiful.

4

The climate was the finest in the world for throat and lung troubles, but on the breaking up of the soil malaria made its appearance and many of the inhabitants suffered from ague and fever. Quinine was the only remedy. There were neither physicians nor trained nurses here, but all were neighbors and friends, always ready to help each other when the occasion required.

In 1856, the year in which Fremont was born, the Pawnee Indians were living four miles south across the Platte river on the bluffs in Saunders county. They numbered about four thousand and were a constant source of annoyance and fear. In winter they easily crossed the river on the ice and in summer the water most of the time was so low they could swim and wade over, consequently there were few days in the year that they did not visit Fremont by the hundred. Weeks and months passed before women and children became accustomed to them and they could never feel quite sure that they were harmless. Stealing was their forte. Eyes sharp and keen were ever on the alert when they were present, yet when they left almost invariably some little article would be missed. They owned buffalo robes and blankets for which the settlers exchanged clothing which they did not need, jewelry, beads, and ornaments, with a little silver coin intermixed. The blankets and robes were utilized for bedding and many were the shivering forms they served to protect from the icy cold of the Nebraska winters. In 1859 the government moved them to another home on the Loup river and in 1876 they were removed to Indian territory.

Snakes of many kinds abounded, but rattlesnakes were the most numerous. They appeared to have a taste for domestic life, as many were found in houses and cellars. A little four-year-old boy one sunny summer day ran out of the house bare-footed, and stepping on the threshold outside the door felt something soft and cold to his feet. An exclamation of surprise caused a member of the household to hasten to the door just in time to see a young rattlesnake gliding swiftly away. In several instances they were found snugly ensconced under pillows, on lounges, and very frequently were they found in cellars.

For more than two years there was no way of receiving or sending mail only as one or another would make a trip to Omaha, which was usually once a week. In 1859 a stage line was put on between Omaha and Fort Kearny. No one can tell with what thankfulness and rejoicing each and every improvement in the condition and surroundings was greeted by the settlers. Dating from the discovery of gold in Colorado the pioneer was no more an object of pity or sympathy. Those who had planted their stakes and made their claims along the old military and California trail were independent. Many of the emigrants became discouraged and turned their faces homeward before getting a glimpse of the Rocky Mountains. On their way home they sold loads of provisions for a song. The same fall the fertile soil of the Platte Valley, after two years of cultivation, responded to the demand of civilization. There was a market west for every bushel of grain and every pound of vegetables grown. So at least the patient and persevering ones received their reward.

The sources of amusement were few, and yet all enjoyed the strange new life. A pleasant ride over the level prairie dotted with wild flowers, in any sort of vehicle drawn by a pair of oxen, was as enjoyable to the young people then as a drive over the country would now be in the finest turnout that Fremont possesses. A dance in a room twelve by sixteen feet in a log cabin, to the music of the Arkansas Traveler played on one violin, was "just delightful." A trip to Omaha once or twice a year was a rare event in the woman's life particularly. Three days were taken, two to drive in and out, and one to do a little trading (not shopping) and look around to view the sights. A span of horses, a lumber wagon with a spring seat in front high up in the air, was the conveyance. Women always wore sunbonnets on these occasions to keep their complexion fair.

Several times in the earlier years the Mormons passed through here with long trains of emigrants journeying to the promised land, and a sorry lot they were, for the most of them were footsore and weary, as they all walked. The train was made up of emigrant

6

covered wagons drawn by oxen, and hand carts drawn by cows, men and women, and dogs. It was a sight never to be forgotten.

This is merely a short description of some of the trials and sufferings endured by the majority of the early settlers of this state. Many of the actors in the drama have passed away, a few only now remaining, and soon the stories of their lives will be to the coming generation like forgotten dreams.

Theron Nye and Mary Colson Nye

Theron Nye, (1828-1901) considered a founding father of the city of Fremont, Nebraska, was born in Brookfield, Madison Co., N.Y., on July 26, 1828 and was brought up on a farm until he was seventeen years of age. He then engaged in various occupations in Madison County, NY until he and his wife located to Fremont, NB, in the Spring of 1857, reportedly with $27.50 in his pocket. There he engaged in farming until he opened the firm of Nye, Colson & Co. in 1866, as dealers in lumber, grain, and agricultural implements. He was joined in this venture by S. B. Colson, James G. and J. T. Smith.

Mr. Nye has the honor of having been the first Mayor of Fremont, serving two terms in that capacity, being first elected in the spring of 1871. He was County Treasurer of his county two terms dating from

*1863 and served as a member of the Board of County Commissioners.
He was also President of the First National Bank of Fremont, NE.*

*He married Miss Caroline M. Colson (1833-1914) in May 1854, in
Hamilton, Madison Co., NY. They had two surviving sons – Fred Nye,
one of the editors of the Omaha Republican, then editor of the Fremont
Tribune and later in New York City as an editor for Joseph Pulitzer's
New York World, and Ray Nye, who served as a bookkeeper for the
above firm Nye, Colson & Co., but rose to become President of the firm,
as it expanded and became the Nye, Schneider, Fowler Company, as well
as serving as President of the Omaha Printing Company.[1]*

---

[1] https://www.findagrave.com/memorial/126166144/theron-nye

RECOLLECTIONS OF THE FIRST SETTLER OF DAWSON COUNTY

BY MRS. DANIEL FREEMAN

I came from Canada to Leavenworth, Kansas. Mr. Freeman was a freighter to Pikes Peak, but was not always successful. He spent $4,000 on one train and came back with only a team of oxen and a team of ponies. The next spring, 1862, I bought a stagecoach and using the pony team, I took my three children, the youngest only two months old, and drove all the way to Nebraska. My husband was there and had started a little store just across from the pony express station on Plum creek. He bought buffalo hides of the Indians and shipped them east. The buffalo were in easy reach and we had fresh meat every day.

We had a big sign with the word "Bakery" on it. I baked a hundred pounds of flour every day. I would make yeast bread over night and bake it in the forenoon, and make salt-rising in the morning and bake it in the afternoon. We got St. Louis flour that the freighters brought from Denver when they came back. I sold my bread for fifty cents a loaf and made as much as thirty dollars a day. I made cheese, too. We had seventy-five head of cows and milked twenty-five. We would take a young calf and let it fill its stomach with its mother's milk, then kill it. Then we took the stomach and washed and wiped it and hung it up on a nail to dry. When it was perfectly dry, we would put it away carefully in a cloth and used it for rennet to make the cheese. I would put a little

9

piece of it in new milk and it would form a solid curd. My husband made me a press and a mold. I got twenty-five cents a pound for my cheese and sold lots of it.

I got up fine meals and charged two dollars a meal. The people were glad to pay it. There was plenty of firewood. The trees drifted down the river and we piled the wood up on the islands, but after the settlers came, they would steal it. There was no need of anybody going hungry those days, for anyone could kill a buffalo. One day a herd of thirty came within ten feet of our door, and our cows went away with them. The children and I walked three miles before we came up to the cows and could get them back home. We were near the river and it was not far down to water. We dug holes in the ground and sunk five salt barrels. The water came up in these and we always had plenty of water. Sometimes we dipped the barrels dry, but they would be full the next morning. There wasn't a pump in the country for years.

The people who kept the Pony Express station were named Humphries. These stations were about fifty miles apart. There would be lots of people at the station every night, for after the Indians became troublesome, the people went in trains of about a hundred wagons. There were many six oxen teams. The Indians never troubled anybody until the whites killed so many buffalo and wasted so much. There were carcasses all over the prairies. The Indians used every part, and they knew this great slaughter of the buffalo meant starvation for them, so they went on the warpath in self-defense. They would skulk on the river bank where the trail came close and would rush up and attack the travelers. The soldiers were sent out as escorts and their families often went with them.

One night at Plum Creek Pony Express station twin babies were born to the lieutenant and wife. I went over in the morning to see if I could help them, but they were all cared for by the lieutenant. He had washed the babies and had the tent in order. I do not remember his name now. We often saw tiny babies with their mothers lying in the wagons that came by. They would be wrapped up and looked very comfortable. Water was so scarce that they had to pay for enough to wash the babies.

Brigham Young made trip after trip with foreign people of all kinds but blacks. Most of these could not speak English, and I don't think Brigham bought any water for them, as they were filthy dirty. Brigham was a great big fat man, and he kept himself pretty neat. He made just about one trip a year. One company of these immigrants was walking through, and the train was a couple of miles long. They went south of the river on the Oregon trail. There was no other road then.

On August 8, 1864, the Sioux people killed eleven men at 11:00 o'clock in the morning, on Elm creek. I was afraid to stay on our ranch, so I took the children and started to Fort Kearny. On the way we came to the place of the massacre. The dead men were lying side by side in a long trench, their faces were covered with blood and their boots were on. Three women were taken prisoners. I heard that there were two children in the party, and that they were thrown in the grass, but I looked all around for them and didn't find any signs of them. Friends of these people wrote to Mr. E. M. F. Leflang, to know if he could locate them. The Indians never troubled us except to take one team during this war, but I was always afraid when I saw the soldiers coming. They would come in the store and help themselves to tobacco, cookies, or anything. Then the teamsters would swing their long black-snake whips and bring them down across my chicken's heads, then pick them up and carry them to camp. I think the officers were the most to blame, for they sold the soldiers' rations, and the men were hungry.

When the Union Pacific railroad was first built, we lived on our homestead north of the river and the town was started on our land. We had the contract to supply the wood for the engines. They didn't use any other fuel then. We hired men to cut the wood on Wood river where Eddyville and Sumner are now. I boarded the men in our new big house across from the depot in old Plum Creek. The store was below and there was an outside stairway for the men to go up. That summer Mr. Freeman was in Washington,

11

Philadelphia, and New York talking up this country. Mr. Freeman was the first county clerk, and his office was upstairs over the store. We rented some of the rooms to newcomers. We did a big business until the railroad moved the town to their section, a mile west. Mr. Freeman kept on trapping, and finally was drowned near Deadwood, South Dakota. I stayed by Dawson county and raised my family, and they all are settled near me and have good homes.

Daniel Freeman, *Plum Creek Nebraska*

Not to be confused with another Daniel Freeman of Nebraska, Mrs. Freeman's husband was born in Michigan, and later lived in Canada. It was there that he met and married his wife, Louisa. They had eight children.[2]

---

[2] https://lexch.com/news/local/plum-creek-s-daniel-freeman/article/July 12 2011

PIONEER JUSTICE

BY B. F. KRIER

In the early history of Lexington, Nebraska, as in all western states, there was no crime committed more reprehensible than that of stealing a horse. One might kill a man and it would be overlooked or excused, but the offense of stealing a horse was a crime that nothing could atone for but the "wiping out" of the thief. And generally, when the horse thief was caught, the nearest tree or the upraised end of a wagon tongue was immediately brought into use as a gallows upon which the criminal was duly hanged without the formalities of courts or juries. It was amply sufficient to know that the accused had stolen a horse, and it mattered but little to whom the horse belonged or whether the owner was present to take a hand in the execution. The culprit was dealt with in such manner that he never stole another animal.

This sentiment prevailed among the first settlers of Dawson county, as was shown in 1871, shortly after the organization of the county. Among the officials of the county at that time was a justice of the peace, a sturdy, honest man, who had been a resident of the county several years before it was organized. One day in 1871 a half-breed Sioux came riding from the east into Plum Creek (as Lexington was then called). The Indian stopped in the town and secured a meal for himself and feed for his horse.

While he was eating, two Pawnee warriors arrived at the station on a freight train, from the east. They at once hunted up the sheriff, a broad-shouldered Irishman named John Kehoe, and made complaint that the half-breed Sioux had stolen a horse from one of

13

them and had the animal in his possession. Complaint was formally made, and a warrant issued for the half-breed's arrest upon the charge of horse-stealing, the warrant being issued by the aforesaid justice of the peace.

The Sioux was at once taken in custody by the sheriff and brought before the justice. One of the Pawnees swore the horse the half-breed rode when he entered the town was his property, and the other Pawnee upon oath declared he knew it was. The prisoner denied the statement made by the Pawnees and vehemently declared the animal was his property; that he came by it honestly, and that the Pawnee had no title whatever in the horse.

There was no jury to hear and judge the evidence, and the justice was compelled to decide the case. He had had some experience with redskins, and entertained but small regard for any of them, but as the preponderance of the evidence was against the Sioux, he decided the latter was guilty, and after a short study of the matter sentenced the culprit to be hanged.

There were no lawyers in Plum Creek at that time, a condition that has not existed since, and each side did its own talking. The Sioux at once filed a vigorous complaint against the sentence but was ordered by the court to keep still.

Realizing he had no chance, he became silent, but some of the citizens who were present and listening to the trial, interposed objections to the strenuous sentence, and informed the court that "as we are now organized into a county and have to go by law, you can't sentence a man to hang fer stealin' a hoss."

This staggered the justice somewhat and he again took the matter under advisement, and shortly after made the following change in the sentence, addressing the prisoner as follows "———, Dem laws don't let you get hanged, vich iss not right. You iss one teef; dat iss a sure thing, and I shust gif you fifteen minutes to git out of dis state of Newbrasky."

The Pawnee secured possession of the horse, but whether it belonged to them or not is questionable, and hit the eastern trail for the "Pawnee house," while the Sioux warrior hastily got himself together and made a swift hike toward the setting sun and safety.

Benjamin F. Krier, proprietor and publisher of Dawson County Pioneer. He located in Plum Creek in 1872, and farmed until 1876, then became connected with the Pioneer. He was born in Montgomery County, PA, August 15, 1855, attended school until he was fifteen, and enlisted in Company D. Third Regiment, New Jersey Volunteer Infantry, in the Third Missouri service; re-enlisted in 1862, in Company G, Tenth New Jersey Volunteer Infantry; served two years; re-enlisted in same company and regiment and participated in all the engagements of U.S. Grant's campaigns from Beaver Dam Station, May 4, 1864, Wilderness, Spotsylvania C.H., and was wounded at Gault House in the face and was discharged November 22, 1864, returned home and learned the printer's trade at which he worked until the spring of 1872, in Trenton and Newark NJ. He then came to Nebraska with the Philadelphia Colony; was married in Trenton, NJ in 1871 to Miss Mary E. Hibbert of the latter place. They have four children, Josephine, Samuel T., Clara H., and Hibbert T. Mr. K. is a member of Thistle Lodge, No. 61 A., F. & A.M. [3]

---

[3] History of the State of Nebraska, 1882, Western Historical Company, A. T. Andreas, Proprietor, Chicago, IL.

EARLY EXPERIENCES IN ADAMS COUNTY

BY GENERAL ALBERT V. COLE

I was a young business man in Michigan in 1871, about which time many civil war veterans were moving from Michigan and other states to Kansas and Nebraska, where they could secure free homesteads. I received circulars advertising Juniata. They called it a village but at that time there were only four houses, all occupied by agents of the Burlington railroad who had been employed to preempt a section of land for the purpose of locating a townsite. In October 1871, I started for Juniata, passing through Chicago at the time of the great fire. With a comrade I crossed the Missouri river at Plattsmouth on a flatboat. The Burlington was running mixed trains as far west as School Creek, now Sutton. We rode to that point, then started to walk to Juniata, arriving at Harvard in the evening. Harvard also had four houses placed for the same purpose as those in Juniata. Frank M. Davis, who was elected commissioner of public lands and buildings in 1876, lived in one house with his family; the other three were supposed to be occupied by bachelors.

We arranged with Mr. Davis for a bed in an upper room of one of the vacant houses. We were tenderfeet from the East and therefore rather suspicious of the surroundings, there being no lock on the lower door. To avoid being surprised we piled everything we could find against the door. About midnight we were awakened by a terrible noise; our fortifications had fallen, and we heard the tramp of feet below. Some of the preemptors had been out on section 37 for wood and the lower room was where they kept the horse feed.

The next morning, we paid our lodging and resumed the journey west. Twelve miles from Harvard we found four more houses placed by the Burlington. The village was called Inland and was on the east line of Adams county but has since been moved east into Clay county. Just before reaching Inland we met a man coming from the west with a load of buffalo meat and at Inland we found C. S. Jaynes, one of the preemptors, sitting outside his shanty cutting up some of the meat. It was twelve miles farther to Juniata, the railroad grade being our guide. The section where Hastings now stands was on the line but there was no town, not a tree or living thing in sight, just burnt prairie. I did not think when we passed over that black and desolate section that a city like Hastings would be builded there. The buffalo and the antelope had gone in search of greener pastures; even the wolf and the coyote were unable to live there at that time.

Six miles farther on we arrived at Juniata and the first thing we did was to drink from the well in the center of the section between the four houses. This was the only well in the district and that first drink of water in Adams county was indeed refreshing. The first man we met was Judson Buswell, a civil war veteran, who had a homestead a mile away and was watering his mule team at the well. Although forty-four years have passed, I shall never forget those mules; one had a crooked leg, but they were the best Mr. Buswell could afford. Now at the age of seventy-three he spends his winters in California and rides in his automobile, but still retains his original homestead.

Juniata had in addition to the four houses a small frame building used as a hotel kept by John Jacobson. It was a frail structure, a story and a half, and when the Nebraska wind blew it would shake on its foundation. There was one room upstairs with a bed in each corner. During the night there came up a northwest wind and every bed was on the floor the next morning. Later another hotel was built called the Juniata House. Land seekers poured into Adams county after the Burlington was completed in July 1872, and there was quite a strife between the Jacobson House and the Juniata House. Finally, a runner for the latter hotel advertised it as the only hotel in town with a cook stove.

Adams county was organized December 12, 1871. Twenty-nine voters took part in the first election and Juniata was made the county-seat.

We started out the next morning after our arrival to find a quarter section of land. About a mile north we came to the dugout of Mr. Chandler. He lived in the back end of his house and kept his horses in the front part. Mr. Chandler went with us to locate our claims. We preempted land on section twenty-eight north of range ten west, in what is now Highland township. I turned the first sod in that township and put down the first bored well, which was 117 feet deep and cost $82.70. Our first shanty was 10x12 feet in size, boarded up and down and papered on the inside with tar paper. Our bed was made of soft-pine lumber with slats but no springs. The table was a flat-top trunk.

In the spring of 1872 my wife's brother, George Crane, came from Michigan and took 80 acres near me. We began our spring work by breaking the virgin sod. We each bought a yoke of oxen and a Fish Brothers wagon, in Crete, eighty miles away, and then with garden tools and provisions in the wagon we started home, being four days on the way. A few miles west of Fairmont we met the Gaylord brothers, who had been to Grand Island and bought a printing press. They were going to publish a paper in Fairmont. They were stuck in a deep draw of mud, so deeply imbedded that our oxen could not pull their wagon out, so we hitched onto the press and pulled it out on dry land. It was not in very good condition when we left it, but the boys printed a very clean paper on it for a number of years.

In August Mrs. Cole came out and joined me. I had broken 30 acres and planted corn, harvesting a fair crop which I fed to my oxen and cows. Mrs. Cole made butter, our first churn being a wash bowl in which she stirred the cream with a spoon, but the butter was sweet, and we were happy, except that Mrs. Cole was very homesick. She was only nineteen years old and a thousand

18

miles from her people, never before having been separated from her mother. I had never had a home, my parents having died when I was very small, and I had been pushed around from pillar to post. Now I had a home of my own and was delighted with the wildness of Nebraska, yet my heart went out to Mrs. Cole. The wind blew more fiercely than now, and she made me promise that if our house ever blew down, I would take her back to Michigan. That time very nearly came on April 13, 1873.

The storm raged three days and nights and the snow flew so it could not be faced. I have experienced colder blizzards but never such a storm as this Easter one. I had built an addition of two rooms on my shanty and it was fortunate we had that much room before the storm for it was the means of saving the lives of four friends who were caught without shelter. Two of them, a man and wife, were building a house on their claim one-half mile east, the others were a young couple who had been taking a ride on that beautiful Sunday afternoon. The storm came suddenly about four in the afternoon; not a breath of air was stirring, and it became very dark. The storm burst, black dirt filled the air, and the house rocked. Mrs. Cole almost prayed that the house would go down so she could go back East. But it weathered the blast; if it had not, I know we would all have perished. The young man's team had to have shelter and my board stable was only large enough for my oxen and cow, so we took his horses to the sod house on the girl's claim a mile away. Rain and hail were falling but the snow did not come until we got home, or we would not have found our way. There were six grown people and one child to camp in our house three days and only one bed. The three women and the child occupied the bed, the men slept on the floor in another room. Monday morning the snow was drifted around and over the house and had packed in the cellar through a hole where I intended to put in a window someday. To get the potatoes from the cellar for breakfast I had to tunnel through the snow from the trap door in the kitchen. It was impossible to get to the well, so we lifted the trap door and melted fresh snow when water was needed.

The shack that sheltered my livestock was 125 feet from the house and it took three of us to get to the shack to feed. Number two would keep within hearing of number one and the third man kept in touch with number two until he reached the stable. Wednesday evening, we went for the horses in the sod house and found one dead. They had gnawed the wall of the house so that it afterwards fell down.

I could tell many other incidents of a homesteader's life, of trials and short rations, of the grasshoppers in 1874-75-76, of hail storms and hot winds; yet all who remained through those days of hardship are driving automobiles instead of oxen and their land is worth, not $2.50 an acre, but $150.

Albert V. Cole, *dealer in general merchandise, was born in Huron County, Ohio, January 14, 1842. His father died March 1842, when Albert was two months old. At six years of age removed with his mother to Canada but remained there only three years, when his mother died; returning to Huron County, and a year later removed to Wayne County, NY and resided on a farm. At seventeen years of age, he went to Lenawee Co., Mich., and farmed until he enlisted on September 12, 1861, in Fourth Michigan Infantry. Was discharged April 1863, and shortly after re-enlisted in Gen. Custer's brigade, Sixth Michigan Cavalry. He was wounded at Cold Harbor, Va., by pistol shot in left arm, which incapacitated him, but he was not discharged until January 6, 1865. During the winter of 1865-1866, he attended Eastman's College at Poughkeepsie, NY, and in the spring of 1867, entered into mercantile business at Addison, MI. One year later he joined Ezra B. Strong, and they conducted the business there until Mr. Cole sold out to come to Nebraska in October 1871. He homesteaded 160 acres in West Blue Precinct, Adams County, residing on the same for over a year. In 1873, he came to Juniata, and engaged in the grocery business, carrying it on alone until he consolidated his business with that of Ira G. Dillon in 1875, and the firm then added general merchandise. On January 1, 1879, Mr. C. purchased his partner's interest, and has since carried the business on alone. He carries a stock of some $10,000 and does an animal business of $20,000 to $25,000. Mr. C. owns some 600 acres of land in the country, which is farmed by renters. He was elected a*

Commissioner of Adams County in the fall of 1879; terms of office three years. He is Captain of Company F, First Regiment Nebraska National Guards, having been commissioned by Gov. Nance in June 1880. Was elected a member of the Board of Trustees of Juniata in April 1880 and re-elected in 1881. Mr. C. was married in Lenawee County, MI September 6, 1869, to Susan P. Crane, a native of Hillsdale County, MI. They have three living children – Lucy J., Ely and Mabel, and one deceased.[4]

---

[4] History of the State of Nebraska, 1882, Western Historical Company, A. T. Andreas, Proprietor, Chicago, IL.

A BROKEN AXLE

BY SAMUEL C. BASSETT

In 1860, Edward Oliver, Sr., his wife and seven children, converts to the Mormon faith, left their home in England for Salt Lake City, Utah. At Florence, Nebraska, on the Missouri river a few miles above the city of Omaha, they purchased a traveling outfit for emigrants, which consisted of two yoke of oxen, a prairie-schooner wagon, and two cows; and with numerous other families having the same destination took the overland Mormon trail up the valley of the Platte on the north side of the river.

When near a point known as Wood River Centre, 175 miles west of the Missouri river, the front axle of their wagon gave way, compelling a halt for repairs, their immediate companions in the emigrant train continuing the journey, for nothing avoidable, not even the burial of a member of the train, was allowed to interfere with the prescribed schedule of travel. The Oliver family camped beside the trail and the broken wagon was taken to the ranch of Joseph E. Johnson, who combined in his person and business that of postmaster, merchant, blacksmith, wagon-maker, editor, and publisher of a newspaper (*The Huntsman's Echo*). Johnson was a Mormon with two wives, a man passionately fond of flowers which he cultivated to a considerable extent in a fenced enclosure. While buffalo broke down his fence and destroyed his garden and flowers, he could not bring himself to kill them. He was a philosopher and, it must be conceded, a most useful person at a point so far distant from other sources of supplies.

The wagon shop of Mr. Johnson contained no seasoned wood suitable for an axle and so from the trees along Wood river was cut an ash from which was hewn and fitted an axle to the wagon and the family again took the trail, but ere ten miles had been traveled the green axle began to bend under the load, the wheels ceased to track, and the party could not proceed. In the family council which succeeded the father urged that they try to arrange with other emigrants to carry their movables (double teams) and thus continue their journey.

The mother suggested that they return to the vicinity of Wood River Centre and arrange to spend the winter. To the suggestion of the mother all the children added their entreaties. The mother urged that it was a beautiful country, with an abundance of wood and water, grass for pasture, and hay in plenty could be made for their cattle, and she was sure crops could be raised. The wishes of the mother prevailed, the family returned to a point about a mile west of Wood River Centre, and on the banks of the river constructed a log hut with a sod roof in which they spent the winter. When springtime came, the father, zealous in the Mormon faith, urged that they continue their journey; to this neither the mother nor any of the children could be induced to consent and in the end the father journeyed to Utah, where he made his home and married a younger woman who had accompanied the family from England, which doubtless was the determining factor in the mother refusing to go.

The mother, Sarah Oliver, proved to be a woman of force and character. With her children she engaged in the raising of corn and vegetables, the surplus being sold to emigrants passing over the trail and at Fort Kearny, some twenty miles distant.

In those days there were many without means who traveled the trail and Sarah Oliver never turned a hungry emigrant from her door, and often divided with such the scanty store needed for her

23

own family. When rumors came of Indians on the warpath the children took turns on the housetop as lookout for the dread savages. In 1863 two settlers were killed by Indians a few miles east of her home. In the year 1864 occurred the memorable raid of the Cheyenne Indians in which horrible atrocities were committed and scores of settlers were massacred by these Indians only a few miles to the south. In 1865 William Storer, a near neighbor, was killed by the Indians.

Sarah Oliver had no framed diploma from a medical college which would entitle her to the prefix "Dr." to her name, possibly she was not entitled to be called a trained nurse, but she is entitled to be long remembered as one who ministered to the sick, to early travelers hungry and footsore along the trail, and to many families whose habitations were miles distant.

Sarah Oliver and her family endured all the toil and privation common to early settlers, without means, in a new country, far removed from access to what are deemed the barest necessities of life in more settled communities.

She endured all the terrors incident to settlement in a sparsely settled locality, in which year after year Indian atrocities were committed and in which the coming of such savages was hourly expected and dreaded. She saw the building and completion of the Union Pacific railroad near her home in 1866; she saw Nebraska become a state in the year 1867. In 1870 when Buffalo county was organized her youngest son, John, was appointed sheriff, and was elected to that office at the first election thereafter. Her eldest son, James, was the first assessor in the county, and her son Edward was a member of the first board of county commissioners and later was elected and served with credit and fidelity as county treasurer.

When, in the year 1871, Sarah Oliver died, her son Robert inherited the claim whereon she first made a home for her family and which, in this year, 1915, is one of the most beautiful, fertile farm homes in the county and state.

Samuel Clay Bassett, *born July 14, 1844 in Delaware County, New York traveled by wagon to Virginia at an early age. After eight years there, his father, Clark, "an anti-slavery Whig, and a reader of the New York Tribune," realized Virginia was not the place to raise a family. Returning to New York state, he purchased a farm in Steuben County. Samuel graduated from Corning Academy in 1861 and probably farmed with his father until his enlistment in Company E, 142nd New York Infantry in 1864. (This may have been 1863 as there are conflicting accounts.) Discharged at the end of the Civil War, Bassett was to continue farming in New York until his departure for Nebraska. He married Lucia M. Baker in 1867 and they had two children when their eyes turned westward.[5]*

[5] *Buffalo Tales*, Buffalo County Historical Society, October 1980, Volume 3, No. 9

EXPERIENCES OF A PIONEER WOMAN

BY MRS. ELISE G. EVERETT

On December 31, 1866, in a bleak wind I crossed the Missouri river on the ice, carrying a nine months' old baby, now Mrs. Jas. Stiles, and my four and a half year old boy trudging along. My husband's brother, Josiah Everett, carried three-year-old Eleanor in one arm and drove the team, and my husband was a little in advance with his team and wagon containing all our possessions. We drove to the town of Decatur, that place of many hopes and ambitions as yet unfulfilled. We were entertained by the Herrick family, who said we would probably remain on Logan creek, our proposed home site, because we would be too poor to move away.

On January 7, 1867, in threatening weather, we started on the last stage of our journey in quest of a home. Nestled deep in the prairie hay and covered with blankets, the babies and I did not suffer. The desolate, wind-swept prairie looked uninviting but when we came to the Logan Valley, it was beautiful even in that weather. The trees along the winding stream, the grove, now known as Fritt's grove, gave a home-like look and I decided I could be content in that valley.

We lived with our brother until material for our shack could be brought from Decatur or Onawa, Iowa. Five grown people and seven children, ranging in ages from ten years down, lived in that small shack for three months. That our friendship was unimpaired is a lasting monument to our tact, politeness, and good nature.

The New Year snow was the forerunner of heavier ones, until the twenty-mile trip to Decatur took a whole day, but finally materials for the shack were on hand. The last trip extended to Onawa and a sled of provisions and two patient cows were brought over. In Decatur, B. S. Roscoe was waiting an opportunity to get to the Logan and was invited to "jump on." It was late, the load was heavy, and somewhere near Blackbird creek the team stuck in the drifts. The cows were given their liberty, the horses unhooked, and with some difficulty the half frozen men managed to mount and the horses did the rest—the cows keeping close to their heels; and so they arrived late in the night. Coffee and a hot supper warmed the men sufficiently to catch a few winks of sleep—on bedding on the floor. A breakfast before light and they were off to rescue the load. The two frozen and dressed porkers had not yet attracted the wolves, and next day they crossed the Logan to the new house.

A few days more and the snowdrifts were a mighty river. B. W. was a sort of Crusoe, but as everything but the horses and cows—and the trifling additional human stock—was strewn around him, he suffered nothing but anxiety. Josiah drove to Decatur, procured a boat, and with the aid of two or three trappers who chanced to be here, we were all rowed over the mile-wide sea, and were at home!

Slowly the water subsided, and Nebraska had emerged from her territorial obscurity (March 1, 1867) before it was possible for teams to cross the bottom lands of the Logan.

One Sunday morning I caught sight of two moving figures emerging from the grove. The dread of Indian callers was ever with me, but as they came nearer my spirits mounted to the clouds—for I recognized my sister, Mrs. Andrew Everett, as the rider, and her son Frank leading the pony. Their claim had been located in March but owing to the frequent and heavy rains we were not looking for them so soon. The evening before we had made out several covered wagons coming over the hills from Decatur, but we were not aware that they had already arrived at Josiah's. The wagons we had seen were those of E. R. Libby, Chas. Morton, Southwell, and Clements.

A boat had brought my sister and her son across the Logan—a pony being allowed to swim the stream but the teams were obliged to go eight miles south to Oakland, where John Oak and two or three others had already settled, and who had thrown a rough bridge across.

Before fall the Andrew Everett house (no shack) was habitable—also a number of other families had moved in on both sides of the Logan, and it began to be a real neighborhood.

One late afternoon I started out to make preparations for the night, as Mr. Everett was absent for a few days. As I opened the door two Indians stood on the step, one an elderly man, the other a much-bedecked young buck. I admitted them; the elder seated himself and spoke a few friendly words, but the smart young man began immediately to inspect the few furnishings of the room. Though quaking inwardly, I said nothing till he spied a revolver hanging in its leather case upon the wall and was reaching for it. I got there first, and taking it from the case I held it in my hands. At once his manner changed. He protested that he was a *good* Indian, and only wanted to *see* the gun, while the other immediately rose from his chair. In a voice I never would have recognized as my own, I informed him that it was time for him to *go*. The elder man at last escorted him outside with me as rear guard. Fancy my feelings when right at the door were ten or more husky fellows, who seemed to propose entering, but by this time the desperate courage of the arrant coward took possession of me, and I barred the way. It was plain that the gun in my hand was a surprise, and the earnest entreaties of my five-year-old boy "not to shoot them" may also have given them pause. They said they were cold and hungry; I assured them that I had neither room nor food for them— little enough for my own babies. At last they all went on to the house of our brother, Andrew Everett. I knew that they were foraging for a large party which was encamped in the grove. Soon they came back laden with supplies which they had obtained, and now they insisted on coming in to *cook them*, and the smell of spirits was so unmistakable that I could readily see that Andrew had judged it best to get rid of them as soon as possible, thinking that they would be back in camp by dark, and the whiskey, which they had obtained between here and Fremont, would have

28

evaporated. But it only made them more insistent in their demands and some were looking quite sullen. At last a young fellow, *not* an Indian—for he had long dark curls reaching to his shoulders—with a strategic smile asked in good English for a "drink of water." Instead of leaving the door, as he evidently calculated, I called to my little boy to bring it. A giggle ran through the crowd at the expense of the strategist, but it was plain they were growing ugly. Now the older Indian took the opportunity to make them an earnest talk, and though it was against their wishes, he at last started them toward the grove. After a while Frank Everett, my nephew, who had come down to bolster up my courage, and the children went to bed and to sleep, but no sleep for me; as the gray dawn was showing in the east, a terrific pounding upon the door turned my blood to ice. Again and again it came, and at last I tiptoed to the door and stooped to look through the crack. A pair of very slim ankles was all that was visible and as I rose to my feet, the very sweetest music I had ever heard saluted me, the neigh of my pet colt Bonnie, who had failed to receive her accustomed drink of milk the previous evening and took this manner of reminding me.

This was the only time we were ever menaced with actual danger, and many laughable false alarms at last cured me of my fears of a people among whom I now have valued friends.

RECOLLECTIONS OF WEEPING WATER, NEBRASKA

BY I. N. HUNTER

Mr. and Mrs. L. D. Hunter were pioneer settlers of Nebraska and Weeping Water, coming from Illinois by team. Their first settlement in the state was near West Point in Cuming county where father staked out a claim in 1857. Things went well aside from the usual hardships of pioneer life, such as being out of flour and having to pound corn in an iron kettle with an iron wedge to obtain corn meal for bread. When the bottom of the kettle gave way as a result of the many thumpings of the wedge, a new plan was devised—that of chopping a hole in a log and making a crude wooden kettle which better stood the blows of the wedge. This method of grinding corn was used until a trip could be made with an ox team, to the nearest mill, forty miles distant; a long and tedious trip always but much more so in this particular instance because of the high water in the streams which were not bridged in those days.

These were small hardships compared to what took place when the home was robbed by Indians. These treacherous savages stripped the premises of all the live stock, household and personal effects. Cattle and chickens were killed and eaten and what could not be disposed of in this way were wantonly destroyed and driven off. Clothing and household goods were destroyed so that little

30

was saved except the clothing the members of the family had on. From the two feather beds that were ripped open, mother succeeded in gathering up enough feathers to make two pillows and these I now have in my home. They are more than a half century old.

A friendly Indian had come in advance of the hostile band and warned the little settlement of the approach of the Indians with paint on their faces. His signs telling them to flee were speedily obeyed and in all probability this was all that saved many lives, as the six or seven families had to keep together and travel all night to keep out of the reach of the Indians until the people at Omaha could be notified and soldiers sent to the scene. On the arrival of the soldiers the Indians immediately hoisted a white flag and insisted that they were "good Indians."

As no one had been killed by the Indians, it was the desire of the soldiers to merely make the Indians return the stolen property and stock, but as much property was destroyed, the settlers received very little. A number of the Indians were arrested and tried for robbing the post office which was at our home. My parents were the principal witnesses and after the Indians were acquitted, it was feared they might take revenge, so they were advised to leave the country.

With an ox team and a few ragged articles of clothing they started east. When he reached Rock Bluffs, one of the early river towns of Cass county, father succeeded in obtaining work. His wages were seventy-five cents a day with the privilege of living in a small log cabin. There was practically no furniture for the cabin, corn husks and the few quilts that had been given them were placed on the floor in the corner to serve as a place to sleep. Father worked until after Christmas time without having a coat. At about this time, he was told to take his team and make a trip into Iowa. Just as he was about to start, his employer said to him: "Hunter, where's your coat?" The reply was, "I haven't any." "Well, that won't do; you can't make that trip without a coat; come with me to the store." Father came out of the store with a new under coat and overcoat, the first coat of any kind he had had since his home was invaded by the red men.

An explanation of the purpose of the trip into Iowa will be of interest. The man father worked for was a flour and meat freighter with a route to Denver, Colorado. In the winter he would go over into Iowa, buy hogs and drive them across the river on the ice, to Rock Bluffs, where they were slaughtered and salted down in large freight wagons. In the spring, from eight to ten yoke of oxen would be hitched to the wagon, and the meat, and often times an accompanying cargo of flour, would be started across the plains to attractive markets in Denver.

Father made a number of these trips to Denver as ox driver.

The writer was born at Rock Bluffs in 1860. We moved to Weeping Water in 1862 when four or five dwellings and the little old mill that stood near the falls, comprised what is now our beautiful little city of over 1,000 population.

During the early sixties, many bands of Indians numbering from forty to seventy-five, visited Weeping Water. It was on one of their visits that the writer made the best record he has ever made, as a foot racer. The seven or eight year old boy of today would not think of running from an Indian, but half a century ago it was different. It was no fun in those days to be out hunting cattle and run onto a band of Indians all sitting around in a circle. In the morning the cattle were turned out to roam about at will except when they attempted to molest a field, and at night they were brought home if they could be found. If not, the search was continued the next day. Some one was out hunting cattle all the time it seemed. With such a system of letting cattle run at large, it was really the fields that were herded and not the cattle. Several times a day some member of the family would go out around the fields to see if any cattle were molesting them. One of our neighbors owned two Shepherd dogs which would stay with the cattle all day and take them home at night. It was very interesting to watch the dogs drive the cattle. One would go ahead to keep the cattle from turning into a field where there might be an opening in

32

the rail fence, while the other would bring up the rear. They worked like two men would. But the family that had trained dogs of this kind was the exception; in most cases it was the boys that had to do the herding. It was on such a mission one day that the writer watched from under cover of some bushes, the passing of about seventy-five Indians all on horseback and traveling single file. They were strung out a distance of almost a mile. Of course they were supposed to be friendly, but there were so many things that pointed to their tendency to be otherwise at times, that we were not at all anxious to meet an Indian no matter how many times he would repeat the characteristic phrase, "Me good Injun." We were really afraid of them and moreover the story was fresh in our minds of the murder of the Hungate family in Colorado, Mrs. Hungate's parents being residents of our vicinity at that time. Her sister, Mrs. P. S. Barnes, now resides in Weeping Water.

Thus, it will be seen that many Indian experiences and incidents have been woven into the early history of Weeping Water.

INCIDENTS AT PLATTSMOUTH

BY ELLA POLLOCK MINOR

Mr. and Mrs. Jacob Vallery were living in Glenwood, Iowa, in 1855, when they decided to purchase a store from some Indians in Plattsmouth. Mr. Vallery went over to transact the business, and Mrs. Vallery was to follow in a few days. Upon her arrival in Bethlehem, where she was to take the ferry, she learned that the crossing was unsafe on account of ice floating in the river. There were two young men there, who were very anxious to get across and decided to risk the trip. They took a letter to her husband telling of the trouble. The next day, accompanied by these two young men, Mr. Vallery came over after her in a rowboat, by taking a course farther north. The boat was well loaded when they started on the return trip. Some of the men had long poles, and by constantly pushing at the ice they kept the boat from being crushed or overturned.

Mrs. Vallery's oldest daughter was the third white child born in the vicinity of Plattsmouth. And this incident happened soon after her arrival in 1855. Mrs. Vallery had the baby in a cradle and was preparing dinner when she heard a knock at the door. Before she could reach it, an Indian had stepped in, and seeing some meat on the table asked for it. She nodded for him to take it, but he seemed to have misunderstood, and then asked for a drink of water. While

Mrs. Vallery was getting the drink, he reached for the baby, but she was too quick for him and succeeded in reaching the baby first. He then departed without further trouble.

At one time the Vallerys had a sick cow, and every evening several Indians would come to find out how she was. She seemed to get no better and still they watched that cow. In the course of a week she died, evidently during the night, because the next morning the first thing they heard was the Indians skinning the cow, out by the shed, and planning a "big feed" for that night down by the river.

The late Mrs. Thomas Pollock used to tell us how the Indians came begging for things. Winnebago John, who came each year, couldn't be satisfied very easily, so my grandmother found an army coat of her brother's for him. He was perfectly delighted and disappeared with it behind the wood pile, where he remained for some time. The family wondered what he was doing, so after he had slipped away, they went out and hunted around for traces of what had kept him. They soon found the clue; he had stuffed the coat in under the wood, and when they pulled it out, they found it was minus all the brass buttons.

Another time one of Mrs. Pollock's children, the late Mrs. Lillian Parmele, decided to play Indian and frighten her two brothers, who were going up on the hill to do some gardening. She wrapped up in cloaks, blankets and everything she could find to make herself look big and fierce, then went up and hid in the hazel brush, where she knew they would have to pass. Pretty soon she peeked out and there was a band of Indians coming. Terrified, she ran down toward her home, dropping pieces of clothing and blankets as she went. The Indians seeing them, ran after her, each one anxious to pick up what she was dropping. The child thinking it was she they were after, let all her belongings go, so she could run the better and escape them. After that escapade quite a number of things were missing about the house, some of them being seen later at an Indian camp nearby.

REMINISCENCES OF CUSTER COUNTY

BY MRS. J. J. DOUGLAS

In July 1888, I arrived at Broken Bow, which is situated geographically about the center of the state. That village looked strange to me with not a tree in sight excepting a few little cuttings of cottonwood and box elder here and there upon a lawn. After having lived all my life in a country where every home was surrounded by groves and ornamental shade trees, it seemed that I was in a desert.

I had just completed a course of study in a normal school prior to coming to Nebraska, and was worn out in mind and body, so naturally my first consideration was the climatic condition of the country and its corresponding effect upon the vegetation. I wondered how the people stood the heat of the day but soon discovered that a light gentle breeze was blowing nearly all the time, so that the heat did not seem intense as it did at my Iowa home.

After I had been in Broken Bow about two weeks, I was offered a position in the mortgage loan office of Trefren and Hewitt. The latter was the first county clerk of Custer county. I held this position a few weeks, then resigned to take charge of the Berwyn school at the request of Mr. Charles Randall, the county superintendent. Berwyn was a village situated about ten miles east of Broken Bow. It consisted of one general merchandise store, a post office, depot, and a blacksmith shop. I shall never forget my first impression on arriving at Berwyn very early on that September morning. It was not daylight when the train stopped at the little depot, and what a feeling of loneliness crept over me as I watched that train speed on its way behind the eastern hills! I found my way to the home of J. O. Taylor (who was then living in the back end of his store building) and informed him that I was the teacher who had come to teach the school and asked him to direct me to my boarding place. Being a member of the school board, Mr. Taylor gave me the necessary information and then sent his hired man with a team and buggy to take me a mile farther east to the home of Ben Talbot, where I was to stay.

The Talbot home was a little sod house consisting of two small rooms. On entering I found Mrs. Talbot preparing breakfast for the family. I was given a cordial welcome, and after breakfast started in company with Mrs. Talbot's little girl for the schoolhouse. The sense of loneliness which had taken possession of me on my way to this place began to be dispelled. I found Mrs. Talbot to be a woman of kind heart and generous impulses. She had two little girls, the older one being of school age. I could see the schoolhouse up on the side of a hill. It was made of sod and was about twelve by fifteen feet. The roof was of brush and weeds, with some sod; but I could see the blue sky by gazing up through the roof at almost any part of it. I looked out upon the hills and down the valley and wondered where the pupils were to come from, as I saw no houses and no evidence of habitation anywhere excepting Mr. Talbot's home. But by nine o'clock about twelve children had arrived from some place, I knew not where.

I found in that little, obscure schoolhouse some of the brightest and best boys and girls it was ever my good fortune to meet. There soon sprang up between us a bond of sympathy. I sympathized with them in their almost total isolation from the world, and they in turn sympathized with me in my loneliness and homesickness.

On opening my school that first morning, great was my surprise to learn how well those children could sing. I had never been in a school where there were so many sweet voices. My attention was particularly directed to the voices of two little girls as they seemed remarkable for children of their years. I often recall one bright sunny evening after I had dismissed school and stood watching the pupils starting out in various directions for their homes, my attention was called to a path that led down the valley through the tall grass. I heard singing and at once recognized the voices of these two little girls. The song was a favorite of mine and I could hear those sweet tones long after the children were out of sight in the tall grass. I shall never forget how charmingly sweet that music seemed to me.

I soon loved every pupil in that school and felt a keen regret when the time came for me to leave them. I have the tenderest memory of my association with that district, though the school equipment was meager and primitive. After finishing my work there, I returned to Broken Bow where I soon accepted a position in the office of J. J. Douglass, clerk of the district court. Mr. Douglass was one of the organizers of Custer county and was chosen the first clerk of the court, which position he held for four years. I began my work in this office on November 16, 1888 and held the position till the close of his term.

During this time many noted criminal cases were tried in court, Judge Francis G. Hamer of Kearney being the judge. One case in which I was especially interested was the DeMerritt case, in which I listened to the testimony of several of my pupils from the Berwyn district. Another far-famed case was the Haunstine case, in which Albert Haunstine received a death sentence. To hear a judge pronounce a death sentence is certainly the most solemn thing one can imagine. Perhaps the most trying ordeal I ever experienced was the day of the execution of Haunstine. It so happened that the scaffold was erected just beneath one of the windows of our office on the south side of the courthouse. As the nails were being driven into that structure how I shuddered as I thought that a human being was to be suspended from that great beam. Early in the morning on the day of the execution people from miles away began to arrive to witness the cruelest event that ever marred the fair name of our beloved state. Early in the day, in company with several others, I visited the cell of the condemned man. He was busy distributing little souvenirs he had made from wood to friends and members of his family. He was pale but calm and self-composed. My heart ached and my soul was stirred to its very depth in sympathy for a fellow being and yet I was utterly helpless so far as extending any aid or consolation. The thought recurred to me so often, why is it men are so cruel to each other—wolfish in nature, seeking to destroy their own kind? And now the thought still comes to me, will the day ever dawn when there will be no law in Nebraska permitting men to cruelly take the life of each other to avenge a wrong? I trust that the fair name of Nebraska may never be blotted again by another so-called *legal* execution.

It was during the time I was in that office the first commencement of the Broken Bow high school was held, the class consisting of two graduates, a boy and a girl. The boy is now Dr. Willis Talbot, a physician of Broken Bow, and the girl, who was Stella Brown, is now the wife of W. W. Waters, mayor of Broken Bow.

We moved our office into the new courthouse in January 1890. Soon after, we saw the completion of the mammoth building extending the entire length of the block on the south side of the public square called the Realty block. The Ansley Cornet band was the first band to serenade us in the new courthouse.

Mr. Douglass completed his term of office as clerk of the district court on January 7, 1892, and two weeks later we were married and went for a visit to my old home in Iowa. Soon after returning to Broken Bow we moved to Callaway. I shall never forget my first view of the little city of which I had heard so much, the "Queen City of the Seven Valleys." After moving to Callaway I again taught school and had begun on my second year's work when I resigned to accept a position in the office of the state land commissioner, H. C. Russell, at Lincoln, where I remained for two years. During the time I was in that office Mr. Douglass was appointed postmaster at Callaway, so I resigned my work in Lincoln and returned home to work in the post office. We were in this office for seven years, after which I accepted a position in the Seven Valleys bank. After a year I again took up school work and have been engaged in that ever since. We have continued to reside at Callaway all these years and have learned to love the rugged hills and glorious sunshine. The winds continue to blow and the sands beat upon our pathway, but we would not exchange our little cottage in the grove for a palace in the far East.

LIFE ON THE FRONTIER

BY JAMES AYRES

Prairie Covered with Indians

In July 1867, a freight train left the old Plum Creek station late one night for the west. As the company was alarmed for the safety of the trains, Pat Delahunty, the section boss, sent out three men on a hand-car over his section in advance of this train. They had gone about three miles to the bend west of the station when they were attacked by Indians. This was at a point nearly north of the John Jacobson claim. There are still on the south side of the track some brickbats near the culvert. This is the place where the Indians built a fire on the south side of the track and took a position on the north side. When the hand-car came along, they fired upon it. They killed one man and wounded another, a cockney from London, England, and thinking him dead, took his scalp. He flinched. They stuck a knife in his neck but even that did not kill him. He recovered consciousness and crawled into the high weeds.

The freight came and fell into the trap. While the Indians were breaking into the cars of the wrecked freight, the Englishman made his escape, creeping a mile to the north. As soon as morning came, Patrick Delahunty with his men took a hand-car and went to investigate. Before they had gone half a mile, they could see the Indians all around the wreck. Each one had a pony.

41

They had found a lot of calico in one car and each Indian had taken a bolt and had broken one end loose and was unfolding it as he rode over the prairie. Yelling, they rode back and forth in front of one another with calico flying, like a Maypole dance gone mad. When they saw the section men with guns, they broke for the Platte river and crossed it due south of where Martin Peterson's house now stands. The section men kept shooting at them but got no game. They found that a squaw-man had probably had a hand in the wrecking of the train for the rails had been pried up just beyond the fire. The smoke blinded the engineer and he ran into the rails which were standing as high as the front of the boiler. The engineer and the fireman were killed. The engine ran off the track, but the cars remained on the rails. The Indians opened every car and set fire to two or three of the front ones. One car was loaded with brick. The writer got a load of these brick in 1872 and built a blacksmith forge. Among the bricks were found pocket knives, cutlery, and a Colt's revolver.

The man who had been scalped came across the prairie toward the section men. They thought he was an Indian. His shirt was gone and his skin was covered with dried blood. They were about to shoot when Delahunty said, "Stop, boys," for the man had his hands above his head. They let him come nearer and when he was a hundred yards away Delahunty said, "By gobs, it's Cockney!" They took him to the section house and cared for him. He told them these details. After this event he worked for the Union Pacific railroad at Omaha. Then he went back to England. The railroad had just been built and there was only one train a day.

Wild Turkeys and Wild Cats

Tom Mahum was the boss herder for Ewing of Texas and had brought his herd up that summer and had his cattle on Dilworth's islands until he could ship them to Chicago. He bantered me for a turkey hunt, and we went on horseback up Plum creek. He was a good shot and we knew we would get game of some kind. We followed the creek five miles, when we scared up a flock of turkeys. They were of the bronze kind, large and heavy. We got three, and as we did not find any more, we took the tableland for the Platte. As we came down a pocket we ran into a nest of wildcats. There were four of them. One cat jumped at a turkey that was tied to Tom's saddle. That scared his horse so that it nearly unseated him, but he took his pistol and killed the cat. I was afraid they would jump at me. They growled and spit, and I edged away until I could shoot from my pony, and when twenty-five yards away I slipped in two cartridges and shot two of the cats. The fourth one got away and we were glad to let it go. We took the three cats to town, skinned them, and sold the pelts to Peddler Charley for one dollar. Tom talked about that hunt when I met him in Oregon a few years ago.

A Scare

On another occasion, Perley Wilson and I took a hunt on the big island south of the river where there were some buffalo. The snow was about eight inches deep and we crossed the main stream on the ice. Before we got over, I saw a moccasin track and showed it to Wilson. He said we had better get out. "No," said I, "let us trail it and find where it goes." It took us into a very brushy island. Wilson would go no further, but I took my shotgun, cocked both barrels, and went on but with caution for fear the Indian would see me first. I got just half way in, and I heard a "Ugh!" right behind me. The hair on my head went straight up. I was scared, but I managed to gasp, "Sioux?" "No, Pawnee. Heap good Indian." Then he laughed and I breathed again. I asked, "What are you doing here?" "Cooking beaver," he replied, and led the way to his fire. He had a beaver skinned hanging on a plum tree and he had a tin can over the fire, boiling the tail. I returned to Wilson and told him about it. He said, "It is no use to try to sneak up on an Indian in the brush, for he always sees you first." I could have shot the Indian, as he only had a revolver, but that would have been cowardly as he had the first drop on me and could have had my scalp. We got home with no game that day.

EARLY RECOLLECTIONS

BY C. CHABOT

After repeated invitations from my old boyhood companion, Dr. Bancroft, to visit him in his new home in western Nebraska, I left Philadelphia and arrived in Omaha the early part of April 1878. Omaha at that time did not impress me very favorably. After buying my ticket to Plum Creek (in those days you could only buy a ticket to Omaha) the next thing in order was to get in line and have my trunk checked, and witness baggage "smashers" demolish a few trunks, then coolly offer to rope them at twenty-five cents each. Our train left at 11 a. m. and arrived in Plum Creek at 11 p. m., good time for those days. The train left with all seats occupied and some passengers standing.

Everybody was eager to see the great prairie country. We expected to see Indians and buffalo, but only a few jack rabbits appeared, which created quite a laugh, as it was the first time any of us had ever seen one run. After we had traveled about twenty miles, "U. P. Sam," as he called himself, came into our car and treated us to a song of his own composition. In his song he related all the wonders of the great Union Pacific railroad and the country between Omaha and Ogden. I saw him two years later in Dawson county, playing the violin at a country dance, and singing songs about different persons at the gathering. All you had to do was to give him a few points as to a man's disposition and habits with a few dimes and he would have the whole company laughing.

We stopped at Grand Island for supper, and in due time arrived in Plum Creek. Dr. Bancroft was waiting for me and after being introduced to many of his western friends, we retired for the night. Next morning, feeling the necessity of visiting a barber shop, I asked the doctor if there was a barber shop in town. Judging from the accommodations at the hotel I had my doubts. "We have a good barber in town," he replied, "but I will go with you."

On arriving at the corner of what is now Main and Depot streets we entered a building which I discovered to be a saloon. I protested, but before I had had time to say much, the doctor asked the barkeeper where Ed. (the barber) was. "Why, he has gone south of the river to plaster a house," was the reply. Then I thought "what kind of a country have I come to, barber and plasterer the same person." Then my mind wandered back to the far East where I saw a comfortable bath room, and I thought "What can the doctor see in this country to deny himself all the comforts of home?" Before I had time to recover from my reveries, I was surrounded by cowboys who insisted that I drink with them. I protested and if it had not been for Dr. Bancroft I suppose they would have made me dance to the music of their six shooters or drink, but as I was a friend of "Little Doc" (as they called him) that was sufficient and the tenderfoot was allowed to leave. Then and only then I saw in the northwest corner of the room the barber's chair.

I accompanied Dr. Bancroft on many drives over the country going as far north as the Loup and Dismal rivers. We went several times south to Arapahoe; in fact, it was but a short time before I was acquainted with most all the settlers in Dawson and adjacent counties. The population at that time was hardly 2,000 in Dawson county. In a very short time, I began to feel more at home. The hospitality of the people was something I had never dreamed of; the climate and good fresh air so invigorating that I soon adjusted myself to surrounding conditions, and before I had been here a month I decided to cast my lot with the rest of the new settlers and became one of them.

While I have had many ups and downs, I cannot say that I regret having done so. When I look back and think of the many friends I made in the early days and how we stood hand in hand in our adversities as well as in our good fortunes, I cannot help feeling that we are more than friends and belong to one big family.

EARLY DAYS IN DAWSON COUNTY

BY LUCY R. HEWITT

Mr. and Mrs. Thomas J. Hewitt, in June 1873, journeyed from Forreston, Illinois, to Plum Creek, Nebraska. Their object was to take advantage of the offer the government was making to civil war soldiers, whereby each soldier could obtain one hundred and sixty acres of land. They stopped at Grand Island and Kearney, but at neither place could they find two adjoining quarter sections, not yet filed on. They wanted two, for my grandfather, Rockwood, who lived with us was also a soldier. At Plum Creek, now Lexington, they were able to obtain what they wanted but it was six miles northwest of the station.

Plum Creek at that early date consisted of the depot. The town was a mile east and when my parents arrived at Plum Creek, they were obliged to walk back to the town, in order to find lodging for the night. Rooms seem to have been scarce for they had to share theirs with another man and his wife. They found a place to eat in the restaurant owned by Mr. and Mrs. E. D. Johnson.

In August of the same year, they made a second trip to Nebraska, this time with wagon and carriage, bringing with others a carpenter who built their house upon the dividing line of the two homesteads. This house had the distinction of being the first two-

47

story house in the neighborhood. All the others were one-story, because the settlers feared the high winds that occasionally swept over the prairies. For a few months it was the farthest away from town.

In the three months between the two trips the town had moved to the depot and had grown from nothing to a village of sixty houses and stores. The Johnsons had brought their restaurant and placed it upon the site where a little later they built a hotel called the Johnson house. Mr. T. Martin had built the first hotel which he named the Alhambra. I have a very faint recollection of being in this hotel when the third trip brought the household goods and the family to the new home. It was in December when this last journey was taken, and great was the astonishment of the older members of the family to see the ground covered with a foot of snow. They had been told that there was practically no winter in Nebraska, and they had believed the statement. They found that the thermometer could drop almost out of sight with the cold, and yet the greater part of many winters was very pleasant.

My father opened a law office in the town and T. L. Warrington, who taught the first school in the village, read law with him, and kept the office open when the farm required attention. The fields were small at first and did not require so very much time.

The first exciting event was a prairie fire. A neighbor's family was spending the day at our farm and some other friends also came to call. The day was warm, no wind was stirring until about 4 o'clock, when it suddenly and with much force blew from the north and brought the fire, which had been smoldering for some days in the bluffs to the north of the farm, down into the valley with the speed of a racing automobile. We children were very much frightened, and grandmother who was sick with a headache, was so startled she forgot her pain—did not have any in fact. Mother and Mrs. Fagot, the neighbor's wife, were outside loosening the tumble weeds and sending them along with the wind before the fire could catch them. In that way they saved the house from catching fire.

My father, who had seen the fire come over the hills as he was driving from town, had unhitched the horses and riding one of them as fast as possible, reached home in time to watch the hay stacks. Three times they caught fire and each time he beat it out with a wet gunny sack. I think this happened in March 1874.

That same year about harvest time the country was visited by grasshoppers. They did considerable damage by nipping off the oat heads before the farmers could finish the reaping. My aunt, who was visiting us, suggested that the whole family walk through the potato field and send the hoppers into the grass beyond. It was a happy thought, for the insects ate grass that night and the next day a favorable wind sent them all away.

The worst grasshopper visitation we had was in July 1876. One Sunday morning father and mother and I went to town to church. The small grain had been harvested and the corn all along the way was a most beautiful, dark green. When we were about a mile from town a slight shade seemed to come over the sun; when we looked up for the cause, we saw millions of grasshoppers slowly dropping to the ground. They came down in such numbers that they clung two or three deep to every green thing. The people knew that nothing in the way of corn or gardens could escape such devastating hordes and they were very much discouraged. To add to their troubles, the Presbyterian minister that morning announced his intention to resign. He, no doubt, thought he was justified.

I was pretty small at that time and did not understand what it all meant, but I do know that as we drove home that afternoon, the cornfields looked as they would in December after the cattle had fed on them—not a green shred left. The asparagus stems, too, were equally bare. The onions were eaten down to the very roots. Of the whole garden, there was, in fact, nothing left but a double petunia, which grandmother had put a tub over. So ravenous were the pests that they even ate the cotton mosquito netting that covered the windows.

In a day or two when nothing remained to eat, the grasshoppers spread their wings and whirred away. Then grandfather said, "We will plant some beans and turnips, there is plenty of time for them to mature before frost." Accordingly, he put in the seeds and a timely rain wet them so that in a very few days they had sprouted and were well up, when on Monday morning, just two weeks and one day from the time of the first visitation, a second lot dropped down and breakfasted off grandfather's beans. It was too late in the season then to plant more.

My mother had quite a flock of turkeys and a number of chickens. They were almost dazed at the sight of so many perfectly good insects. They tried to eat them all but had to give up the task. They ate enough, however, to make themselves sick.

This time I believe the grasshoppers stayed several days. They seemed to be hunting some good hard ground in which to lay their eggs. The following spring the warm days brought out millions of little ones, which a prairie fire later destroyed.

The corn crop having been eaten green and the wheat acreage being rather small, left many people with nothing to live on during the winter. Many moved away and many of those who could not get away had to be helped. It was then that Dawson county people learned that they had good friends in the neighboring states for they sent carloads of food and clothing to their less fortunate neighbors.

A good many homesteaders were well-educated, refined people from Pennsylvania, New York, and elsewhere. They were a very congenial company and often had social times together. They were for the most part young people, some with families of young children, others just married, and some unmarried. I remember hearing my mother tell of a wedding that she and father attended. The ceremony was performed at a private house and then the whole company adjourned to a large hall where everybody who wanted to danced, and the rest watched until the supper was served by Mr. and Mrs. Johnson in their new hotel. The bride on this occasion was Miss Addie Bradley and the groom was W. H. Lingle, at one time county superintendent of public instruction.

For some time after the starting of the town of Plum Creek there was no church edifice but there was a good sized schoolhouse, and here each Sunday morning the people for miles around gathered. One Sunday the Methodist preacher talked to all the people and the next week the Presbyterian minister preached to the same congregation, until the courthouse was built, and then the Presbyterians used the courtroom. I have heard the members say that they received more real good from those union services than they ever did when each denomination had a church of its own. The Episcopalians in the community were the most enterprising for they built the first church, a little brick building that seated one hundred people. It was very plainly furnished, but it cost fifteen hundred dollars, due to the fact that the brick was brought from Kearney and freight rates were high. It stood on the site of the present modern building and was built in 1874. My grandfather, an ardent Churchman, often read the service when there was no rector in town.

Speaking of the courthouse reminds me that it was not always put to the best use. I cannot remember when the following incident occurred, but I do remember hearing it talked of. A man who lived on the south side of the Platte river was accused of poisoning some flour that belonged to another man. He was ordered arrested and two or three men, among them Charles Mayes, the deputy sheriff, were sent after him. He resisted arrest and using his gun, killed Mayes. He was finally taken and brought to town and put into the county jail in the basement of the courthouse. Mayes had been a very popular man and the feeling was very high against his slayer, so high, indeed, that some time between night and morning the man was taken from the jail, and the next morning his lifeless body was found hanging at the back door of the courthouse.

One of the pleasures of the pioneer is hunting. In the early days there was plenty of game in Dawson county, buffalo, elk, deer, antelope, jack rabbits, and several game birds, such as plover, prairie hen, ducks, geese, and cranes. By the time we arrived, however, the buffalo had been driven so far away that they were seldom seen. There was plenty of buffalo meat in the market,

51

however, for hunters followed them and shot them, mostly for their hides. The meat was very good, always tender and of fine flavor. My father rushed into the house one day and called for his revolver. A herd of buffalo was racing across the fields towards the bluffs on the north. Father, and some of the men with him, thought possibly they might get near enough to shoot one. But although he rode as fast as his pony could carry him, he could not get close enough and the herd, once it reached the hills was safe. The poor beasts had been chased for miles and were weary, but they did not give up. The cows huddled the calves together and pushed them along and the bulls led the way. Father learned afterward that his pony had been trained by the Indians to hunt; and if he had given him the rein and allowed him to go at it in his own way, he would have gone so close that father could have shot one. But he did not know this until the buffalo were far away.

A GRASSHOPPER STORY

BY MARGARET F. KELLY

I came to Fremont, Nebraska, in May 1870, and settled on a farm on Maple creek. In 1874 or 1875 we were visited by grasshoppers. I had never formed an idea of anything so disastrous. When the "hoppers" were flying the air was full of them. As one looked up, they seemed like a severe snow storm. It must have been like one of the plagues of Egypt. They were so bad one day that the passenger train on the Union Pacific was stalled here. I went to see the train and the odor from the crushed insects was nauseating. I think the train was kept here for three hours. The engine was besmeared with them. It was a very wonderful sight. The rails and ground were covered with the pests. They came into the houses and one lady went into her parlor one day and found her lace curtains on the floor, almost entirely eaten.

Mrs. George Turner said that she came home from town one day when the "hoppers" were flying and they were so thick that the horses could not find the barn. Mrs. Turner's son had a field of corn. W. R. Wilson offered him fifty dollars for it. When he began to husk it, there was no corn there. A hired man of Mrs. Turner's threw his vest on the ground. When he had finished his work and picked up the vest it was completely riddled by the grasshoppers. I heard one man say that he was out riding with his wife and they stopped by a field of wheat where the "hoppers" were working and they could hear their mandibles working on the wheat. When they flew it sounded like a train of cars in motion. Horses would not face them unless compelled.

One year I had an eighty acre field of corn which was being cultivated. The men came in and said the "hoppers" were taking the corn. They did not stay long, but when they left no one would have known that there had ever been any corn in that field. My brother from California came in 1876. On the way to the farm a thunder storm came up and we stopped at a friend's until it was over. My brother said, "I would not go through the experience again for $10,000, and I would not lose the experience for the same amount." The "hoppers" came before the storm and were thick on the ground. It was a wonderful experience.

In those days we cut our small grain with "headers." The grain head was cut and fell into boxes on wagons. After dinner one day, the men went out to find the grasshoppers in full possession. A coat which had been left hanging was completely destroyed. Gardens and field crops were their delight. They would eat an onion entirely out of the hard outer skin. I had a thirty acre field of oats which looked fine on Saturday. We could not harvest it then and on Monday it looked like an inverted whisk broom. Some of the "hoppers" were three inches long. The backs were between brown and slate color and underneath was white. I think we received visits from them for five years.

Margaret Kelly was a historian with the Lewis and Clark chapter of the Daughters of the American Revolution.

PIONEERING IN FILLMORE COUNTY

BY JOHN R. MCCASHLAND

In the fall of 1870, with Mrs. McCashland and two children, Addie and Sammy, I left Livingston county, Illinois, and drove to Fillmore county, Nebraska. We started with two wagons and teams. I had three good horses and one old plug. I drove one team and had a man drive the other until I became indignant because he abused the horses and let him go. Mrs. McCashland drove the second team the rest of the way.

A family of neighbors, Thomas Roe's, were going west at the same time, so we were together throughout the journey until we got lost in the western part of Iowa. The road forked and we were so far behind we did not see which way Roe turned and so went the other way. It rained that night, and a dog ate our supplies, so we were forced to procure food from a settler. We found the Roe family the next evening just before we crossed the Missouri river, October 15, 1870.

East of Lincoln we met a prairie schooner and team of oxen. An old lady came ahead and said to us, "Go back, good friends, go back!" When questioned about how long she had lived here, she said, "I've wintered here and I've summered here, and God knows I've been here long enough."

When Mrs. McCashland saw the first dugout that she had ever seen, she cried. It did not seem that she could bear to live in a place like that. It looked like merely a hole in the ground.

We finally reached the settlement in Fillmore county and lived in a dugout with two other families until I could build a dugout that we could live in through the winter. That done, I picked out my claim and went to Lincoln to file on it and bought lumber for a door and for window frames.

I looked the claim over, chose the site for buildings, and when home drew the plans of where I wanted the house, stable, well, etc., on the dirt hearth for Mrs. McCashland to see. She felt so bad because she had to live in such a place that I gave it up and went to the West Blue river, which was near, felled trees, and with the help of other settlers hewed them into logs and erected a log house on the homestead. While living in the dugout, Indian women visited Mrs. McCashland and wanted to trade her a papoose for her quilts. When she refused, they wanted her to give them the quilts.

I had just forty-two dollars when we reached Fillmore county, and to look back now one would hardly think it possible to live as long as we did on forty-two dollars. There were times that we had nothing but meal to eat and many days we sent the children to school with only bread for lunch.

I was a civil war veteran, which fact entitled me to a homestead of one hundred and sixty acres. I still own that homestead, which is farmed by my son. After visiting in the East a few years ago I decided that I would not trade my quarter section in Fillmore county for several times that much eastern land.

John Ruby McCashland (1841-1917) was born May 4, 1841, in Mayne Co., Indiana. In his infancy, his parents moved to Neoska Co., Indiana, here they lived until he was eleven years old. The family then in 1852 moved to Livingston, Co., Ill, where at the age of fifteen, he was converted and joined the Methodist Church and remained a member of the church to the time of his death. At the age of twenty, he enlisted in Company A, 43rd Illinois Infantry and served continuously for four years as a private, corporal, sergeant, and at the close of the war was discharged as first sergeant of his Company. His discharge reads July 22, 1865. After the war he returned to his home neighborhood and resumed farming.

August 23, 1866, he was united in marriage to Amanda Houchin in Livingston Co., Ill. October 16, 1870 Mr. and Mrs. MCashland landed in Fillmore Co., Nebraska. To this union were born seven children. At the age of seventy-six years, Mr. McCashland passed away.[6]

[6] https://www.findagrave.com/memorial/54632787/john-ruby-mccashland

REMINISCENCES OF GAGE COUNTY

BY ALBERT L. GREEN

The writer has in his possession an old map of the North American continent published in London in 1796, twelve years after the close of the American Revolution, whereon the region now comprising the state of Nebraska is shown as a part of Quivera; that supposed kingdom of fabulous riches in quest of which Coronado pursued his tedious wanderings more than three hundred years ago. At the time this map was published the French had visited Indian tribes as far west as the Missouri, and it must have been from French and Spanish sources that the geographer and map-maker gathered the information that enabled him to compile that part of his map covering the vast unknown regions of the west.

Guess-work and supposition resulted in elongations and abbreviations of territory and rivers that made it possible for him to show our own Blue river as emptying into the Gulf of California, and the great kingdoms of Quivera and Teguayo as extending from the Missouri river to the Pacific coast. The greater part of what is now Mexico is shown as "New Biscay" and "New Navarre," while Mexico or "New Spain" is crowded down towards Central America. The existence of the Rocky Mountains, at the time this map was made, was unknown; and the whole region covered by them is shown as a vast plain.

While spending leisure hours among some rare old books in the library of the Union League of Philadelphia, I came across the chronicles of Coronado's wanderings and adventures, as detailed by his monkish chaplain and preserved in the Spanish archives. A careful perusal of these fully convinced me that the route traversed was through eastern Nebraska as far northward as the present site of Lincoln, and possibly as far as the Platte. The great salt marsh was referred to, and the particulars of a disastrous encounter with the warlike Otoes are given. Mention is made of the Missouri nation and its bold warriors, as well as of other tribes whose habitat and hunting grounds were the plains or prairies of eastern Nebraska.

In prehistoric times the Indian trails led along the level river bottoms where both wood and water could be obtained and where game was usually most abundant, and also in the direction of salt springs or licks where salt might be obtainable and the larger kinds of game be more plentiful. At the time of its settlement by white people the bottom lands of the Blue were threaded by many deeply worn trails that had evidently been traveled for centuries and a careful consideration of happenings, as recorded by the monkish chronicler, and the fact I have just stated in regard to the prehistoric routes of travel, forces the conclusion that Coronado's weary cavalcade must undoubtedly have followed the course of the Blue river to a point where the well worn trail diverged towards the great salt basin. Possibly the party may have encamped on the site of Beatrice, and there can be little doubt that one of the Indian cities mentioned by the faithful monkish historian occupied the present site of Blue Springs, where evidences of an ancient Indian town can still be seen, and the outlines of ancient fortifications be traced.

Fragments of Indian pottery and stone knives and implements, of both the paleolithic and the Neolithic ages, are frequently turned up by the plowshare in that vicinity, all indicating a long established occupancy that must have continued for centuries. As late as the early part of the last century the Pawnees occupied the site; and when the writer, as United States government agent, took charge of the Otoes and Missouris, in the summer of 1869, there were still old warriors living who remembered hearing their fathers tell of deeds of bloody warfare done in this very vicinity, and who pointed out to the writer the very spot, in a deep draw or ravine on the prairie a few miles east of Blue Springs, where a war party of thirty Otoes met a well-deserved, but terrible death. At the time of this occurrence the Otoes were living at the mouth of the Nemaha and were on very bad terms with the Pawnees, many of whose scalps the writer has seen adorning Otoe medicine bags or hanging in their wigwams.

The Pawnees had started on a buffalo hunt, leaving at home only the old and decrepit and a few children, and the Otoes, knowing that the defenders of the village had started on the hunt, made an attack at daybreak the next morning, murdering and scalping old and young alike, and after loading themselves with plunder, hastened on their homeward trip. Unfortunately for the Otoes the Pawnee hunters had encamped only eight miles up Indian creek and one of them that morning had returned to the village on some errand and arrived just in time to discover what was going on. The Otoes wounded him severely, but he succeeded in escaping to the Pawnee camp and giving the alarm.

The enraged Pawnee warriors, mounted on their freshest and fastest ponies, were not long in reaching the village, nor were they long in discovering the trail of the Otoe war party, which they followed until they overtook it at the place pointed out to the writer. Here a fierce battle took place which resulted in the complete extermination of the Otoe party; the tall slough grass, in which they took shelter, having been set on fire, the wounded all perished in the conflagration. This is probably one of the most tragic incidents of which we have any knowledge as having happened within the limits of Gage county.

The first store established within the county was located in a log house on Plum creek near the present site of the village of Liberty. It was established, primarily as an Indian trading place, by a Mr. MacDonald, of St. Joseph, Missouri, but was under the management of Mrs. Palmer, who with her husband, David, were the first white settlers within the limits of the county, having arrived in 1857 a few weeks prior to the coming of the founders of Beatrice. David was drowned a few years ago while bathing in the Blue. The store on Plum creek, on one occasion, was raided by a party of Pawnees who, loaded with plunder, were pursued by a large party of Otoes, who overtook them on the Little Blue some distance above the present site of Fairbury, and killed them all. The site of this battle was pointed out to the writer by the Otoes while accompanying them on a buffalo hunt in 1870. The skulls and bones of the slain were still in evidence at that time, being concealed in the dense thicket in which the battle had taken place.

About the year 1868 a war party of Osages made a raid on the aboriginal inhabitants of the county and murdered and scalped several squaws who were chopping wood near the Blue. The trail of the Osages was followed, by a war party of Otoes, to the reservation of the former and satisfaction exacted in the shape of a gift of forty head of ponies. On their way back the Otoes concluded that they had settled too cheaply and feared they might be censured by the kindred of the murdered women. They halted, and leaving the forty head of ponies under guard, made a flying raid on the Osage pony herds and succeeded in stealing and getting safely away with another forty head. In due time, with eighty head of Osage ponies, they made a triumphal daylight entry into their home village. If they had been unsuccessful, they would have stolen in one by one during the darkness of the night.

The last Indian war party to traverse the soil of Gage county consisted of thirty naked and painted Omahas. It transpired that a party of Kickapoos had raided the pony herds of the Omahas and stolen thirty head of ponies, and in order to throw suspicion on the Otoes, had cunningly directed their trail towards the Otoe reservation, passing in the night as near to the Otoe village as

61

possible without being discovered. The Otoes at this time were expecting, and trying to guard against, a raid from the Osages, whom they had great reason to fear, as it was fully expected that they would exact satisfaction, sooner or later, for that extra forty head of ponies that the Otoes had stolen.

As a protection from the Osages, the Otoes had constructed a sort of a stockade of poles tied together with withes and strips of bark, in front of each wigwam, where they kept their nearly eight hundred head of ponies under careful watch every night. The Omaha war party stealthily approached under cover of the darkness and finding sentinels posted and watching, they hid in the tall weeds and sunflowers as close to the stockades as they could safely get, until daybreak, when the sleepy sentinels, thinking all danger over, entered the wigwams for something to eat and a nap, then emerging from their hiding places the Omahas made quick work of cutting the lashings that bound the poles and selecting thirty of the best ponies they could get hold of. The noise of the ponies' hoof-beats, as the Omahas rode swiftly away, aroused the Otoes, and in a very few minutes the whole village was in a commotion.

Fierce war whoops resounded; the heralds went about calling the braves into action and soon there was mounting in hot haste. The writer, awakened by the tumult, stepped out upon a balcony in front of the agency building and beheld a sight such as no historian of the county will ever again record. In the far distance the naked Omahas were riding for their very lives, while perhaps a hundred or more Otoes were lashing their ponies in a wild frenzy of pursuit. In the village the greatest commotion prevailed, the women wailed, the heralds shouted, and the dogs barked; scores of women stood on the tops of their wigwams shrieking and gesticulating and the temper of the community closely resembled that of a nest of hornets when aroused by the rude thrust of a pole.

It was nearly noon when the distant war whoops, announcing the return of the pursuers, were heard; as they drew near it was apparent that they were wildly triumphant and were bringing with them the thirty hideously painted Omahas. The prisoners were delivered to the agent who directed his police to disarm them, and cause them to be seated on the floor of the council room where they formed a dejected looking group with their naked bodies and shaved and vermillion painted heads. It was then that their leader explained that their seizure of ponies was honestly intended as a reprisal for ponies which they had lost. Old Medicine Horse, an Otoe chief, assured them that his braves would have killed every one of them if the agent had not talked so much about the wickedness of killing, and it was only their fear of displeasing him that caused them to take prisoners instead of scalps. After much speech-making, the agent adjourned the council and suggested that the Otoes take the Omahas to their wigwams, feed them, and allow them to depart in peace; and this was done. The only blood shed during the campaign was in the shooting of one of Elijah Filley's hogs by the Omahas. The first notification I had of this atrocious and bloody affair was when Elijah, then quite a young man, came to see me and file a complaint, bringing with him the blood-stained arrow that had pierced the vitals of his innocent hog.

Perhaps one of the saddest tragedies of those early days occurred in 1870 when two homesteaders, returning to their families from a trip to Brownville for provisions, were brutally murdered by a half-breed named Jim Whitewater. Jim was just returning from a buffalo hunt and had secured a supply of whiskey from a man named Wehn, at Fairbury. Being more than half drunk, he conceived the idea that the bravest thing he could do would be to kill some white people; and it happened that he came across the poor homesteaders just at that time. It was about dusk, and the poor fellows had halted for the night, by the side of a draw where the grass was tall enough to cut for their horses. They had unharnessed their teams, tied them to the wagons and were in the act of mowing grass for them when a pistol shot rang out and one of them fell mortally wounded; the other, being attacked, and though mortally hurt, tried to defend himself with the scythe that he had been using, and in doing so cut the Indian's hand, almost severing the thumb. The scene of this terrible affair was just over the Gage county line in Jefferson county and consequently it

63

devolved on the sheriff of that county to discover and arrest the murderer. As Whitewater had been seen in the vicinity, suspicion pointed to him and his arrest followed. He soon escaped from the officers and was hidden for two weeks, when the Indian police discovered his place of concealment in the timber on Wolf creek. His own brother, assisted by other Indians, captured him by strategy, bound him securely with their lariats and delivered him at the agency.

The writer had gone to Beatrice on business and was not expected back until the next day, but in his absence his wife, then a young woman of about twenty, took energetic measures to insure the safety of the prisoner by ordering him placed in irons, and kept under a strong guard until the agent's return. In the meantime, having finished the business at Beatrice and there being a full moon, the writer decided to drive the twenty miles to the agency between sundown and midnight, which he did, arriving there shortly after midnight. Of course, until his arrival, he had no intimation that Whitewater had been captured.

Before leaving home the Indians had reported that they had reason to believe that he was hiding somewhere on Wolf creek, as his wife had taken dried buffalo meat to that locality, and as the writer, in returning, had to drive for about forty rods through the heavy timber bordering that creek and cross it at a deep and rather dangerous ford, and knowing that Whitewater had declared that he would take both the agent and the sheriff with him to the other world, and that he was heavily armed, the writer is not ashamed to confess to a feeling of nervousness almost akin to fear, as he was about to enter that stretch of timber shaded road dimly lighted by the full moon. He first carefully let down the curtains of the carriage and then made his team dash at full speed through the long stretch of timber, plunge and flounder through the ford, and out once more upon the open prairie, the driver expecting at almost any moment to hear the crack of a pistol.

On arriving within sight of the agency building, instead of finding it dark and silent as he had expected, the writer was greatly surprised to see it well lighted and many Indian police standing about it as if on guard. The next morning the writer with several Indian chiefs and the Indian police started for Fairbury with the prisoner; the Indians riding two abreast and carrying a large United States flag at the head of the procession. The trip was made via Beatrice and the distance traveled was about fifty miles. The Indians feared an attack from the Rose creek settlers; neighbors and friends of the murdered men, and as they approached Fairbury the entire line of Indians commenced a melodious chant which the interpreter explained as nothing less than an appeal to the Great Spirit asking him to incline the hearts of the people to treat the Indians kindly and fairly. On arriving at Fairbury, the cavalcade halted in the public square and was soon surrounded by the entire population of the hamlet. It was nearly dark, but the good ladies of the place set about preparing a bountiful meal for the hungry Indians, to which they did ample justice.

There being no jail in the place, we waived a hearing and started the next morning for Pawnee City, where prison accommodations could be had. Shortly after leaving Fairbury the interpreter told the Indians that evidently the Great Spirit had heard their appeal, to which they all vociferously assented. Jim was kept at Pawnee City until his trial, which took place at Fairbury before Judge O. P. Mason, who sentenced him to imprisonment for life.

Whitewater was one of three individuals among the Otoes who could read and write, the other two being Battiste Barneby and Battiste Deroin, both of whom were very capable interpreters. Polygamy being allowable among the Otoes, Deroin was one who had availed himself of its privileges, his two wives being sisters. On learning that Whitewater had been imprisoned for life, his wife soon found another husband, greatly to his sorrow and chagrin. It was during Whitewater's imprisonment that the reservation was sold, and the Indians removed. Eighteen years after his conviction he received a pardon and left the penitentiary to rejoin the tribe. What retribution he meted out to those who aided in his capture or to his wife's second husband, the writer has never learned.

A year before the writer took charge of the Otoes and Missouris, a delegation of their chiefs had accompanied their agent Major Smith, to Washington and made a treaty under which the whole reservation of 160,000 acres was to be sold at $1.50 per acre. The writer was informed by Major Smith that a railroad company would become the ultimate beneficiary, provided the treaty was ratified by the senate, and that he had been promised a section of land if the scheme proved successful. Smith urged the writer to use all the influence possible to secure the ratification of the treaty and before the writer had taken any steps to secure its defeat, he also received an intimation, if not an absolute promise, from interested parties, that in the event of its ratification, he should have his choice of any section of land on the domain. Believing that such a treaty was adverse to the interests and welfare of the Indians, the writer at once set about to accomplish its defeat, in which, through the aid of eastern friends, he was finally successful.

Coronado's chronicler mentions, among other nations with whom the expedition came in contact, the *Missourias* as being very fierce and warlike, and it may be a matter of local historical interest to state that the Missouri "nation" with which Coronado became acquainted, and from which one of the world's largest rivers and one of the largest and richest states take their names, reduced to a remnant of less than one hundred individuals, found an abiding place within the limits of Gage county for more than a generation. Placed on a reservation with the Otoes and under the care of the same agent, they still retained their own chief and their own language, though circumstances gradually induced the adoption of the Otoe tongue.

The old chief of the Missouris was called Eagle and was known as a war chief. It was his province to command and direct all hunting operations. He was a man of very striking appearance, over six feet in height, straight as an arrow, with fine features and apparently about seventy-five years of age in 1869. He was an hereditary chief, and probably a lineal descendant of one of the kings of the Missouri nation that Coronado and his followers met.

Old Eagle was the only chief of the Missouris, and was respected and highly esteemed by both the Missouris and the Otoes. During a buffalo hunt, in which the writer participated with the Indians, Eagle chief was the highest authority in regard to all matters pertaining to the chase and attack on the herd. In 1869 the head chief of the Otoes was Arkeketah who was said to have been appointed to that position by Major Daily. He was a polygamist and very much opposed to the ways of the white man. In fact, he was such a reactionary and stumbling-block to the progress of the tribe that the writer finally deposed him and advanced Medicine Horse to the position of head chief.

The number of Indians living within the borders of Gage county in 1869 was probably not far from eight hundred. The reservation, comprising two hundred and fifty square miles, extended some distance into Kansas and also took in a part of Jefferson county in this state, but the Indians were all domiciled in Gage county. Their principal village was situated close to the site now occupied by the town of Barnston and where a fine spring afforded an ample supply of water. The wigwams were of a type adopted by the Indians long before the discovery of America, and most of them were large enough to accommodate several families. It was a custom of the Otoes to vacate the wigwams and live during the winter in tipis which were pitched in the timber where fuel was close at hand. In 1869 only three persons in the confederated tribes wore citizens clothes, the rest were all blanket Indians, who, during warm weather, went almost naked, and habitually painted their faces and shaved heads, with vermillion and indigo.

The principal burial place of the Otoes was on a bluff overlooking the river bottoms, and within a short distance of where Barnston now stands. For years it was visited, as one of the curiosities of the reservation, by the white settlers and strangers, chiefly on account of the weird and ghostly funeral oaks that stood on the brink of the bluff, bearing, lashed to their gnarled and crooked limbs, gruesome burdens of dead Indians, wrapped in bark and partly mummified by the sun and wind; there was probably a score of these interesting objects resting peacefully on the boughs of these three oaks; they had been there for many years, and might possibly have remained to this day had not a great prairie fire during the summer of 1871 destroyed the oaks and their ghastly burden, leaving only an assortment of charred bones and skulls to mark the site.

A strange and pathetic tragedy, in connection with this old burial place, transpired shortly before the writer took charge of the agency and its affairs; and it was from the interpreter, Battiste Deroin, that the particulars were obtained. The incident may be worth preserving by the local historian, as illustrating the absolute faith of the Indians in a continued existence of the spirit beyond the grave. Dogs were frequently strangled at children's funerals in order that the dog's spirit might accompany that of the child, and it was a common sight to see a dog's body sitting upright with its back to a stake and securely tied in that position, in the vicinity of the old burial place. The man who figured in this tragedy was very aged and feeble, and the little child was very dear to him; he doubtless knew that he had not long to live and that he very soon would have to travel over the same lonely trail that the little child was about to take. Doubtless he realized fully what a comfort it would be to each if they could take the long journey together. The Otoes always buried their dead in a sitting posture; and the old man, when seated in the grave, held the body of the child in his arms. The relatives took a last farewell of both the dead child and its living caretaker; the grave was covered with a buffalo robe supported on poles or heavy sticks, and the mass of earth taken from the grave was piled thereon; this being their usual mode of burial.

The custom of strangling a horse or pony at the burial of an Indian brave was a common occurrence among the Otoes prior to 1870 and the old burial place on the bluff was somewhat decorated with horses' skulls laid upon the graves of warriors who are supposed to have gone to heaven on horseback. The tail of the horse sacrificed was usually fastened to a pole that stood at the head of the grave.

68

The first school established within the limits of the county was a mission school under the care of the Rev. Mr. Murdock, and the old stone building, built for it on Mission creek, was the first stone building in the county. It was a ruin in 1869.

In 1869 there were still some beavers to be found along the Blue; and at that time the river abounded with large gars, some of which were three or four feet in length; a fish which has since become entirely extinct in the Blue, probably because the water is no longer clear. The gar was one of the primitive fishes of the Silurian age; it was very destructive of all other fish. White people never ate it, but the Indians thought it fairly good. The Indians obtained most of their fish by shooting with arrows from the river banks. They often succeeded in shooting very large fish owing to the clearness of the water. This could not be done now that the prairies have been put into cultivation, as that has destroyed the clearness of the water.

As late as 1869 there were some wild deer in the county and little spotted fawns were occasionally caught. The writer procured two of the latter from the Indians and gave them to Ford Roper's family in Beatrice; they became very tame and were frequently seen on the streets of the town. In 1870 the writer, while driving from Blue Springs to Beatrice, met a large buck with antlers, as it emerged from an opening in the bluffs.

Among the first settlers of the county were some families from Tennessee who settled near the present town of Liberty on Plum creek. They did their own spinning and weaving and having been accustomed to raising cotton and mixing it with the wool for spinning, they undertook to raise it here. The writer remembers seeing their cotton patches, but never saw them gathering cotton.

The first bridge built in the county to cross the river, was built on Market street, Beatrice, about the year 1870. It was a very narrow wooden structure, only wide enough for one wagon at a time to pass over. The firm of Peavy and Curtiss of Pawnee City were the contractors, and the contract price was $4,000. It was regarded as a public improvement of very great importance to the town.[7]

Albert Lampton Green (1845-1947) *Green was born in Pennsylvania in 1845. In 1869, President Grant adopted the policy of putting the administration of Indian reservations into the hands of members of the Society of Friends or Quakers. Green, a Quaker, was appointed agent of the Otoe tribe, whose home was in Gage County near where the town of Barneston now stands. Green's term as agent ended in 1872 and he was given the choice to continue as agent with the Otoe tribe or accept the same position with the Winnebagos. Instead, Green and his wife chose to move to the young town of Beatrice with his new daughter. Green and his wife, Sallie Cadwallader Lightfoot, raised four children in Beatrice. A. L. Green remained a resident of Beatrice, working in real estate, until his death on February 25, 1947.*

---

[7]

https://nebraskahistory.pastperfectonline.com/byperson?keyword=Green%2C+Albert+Lamborn%2C+1845-1947

RANCHING IN GAGE AND JEFFERSON COUNTIES

BY PETER JANSEN

I came to Beatrice, Nebraska, in 1874, after having been through Minnesota, Dakota, and Kansas, looking for a place where a settlement of our people, the Mennonites, could be established. Of all the land I had looked over, I liked southeastern Nebraska best, and the little town of Beatrice on the banks of the Big Blue, then consisting of maybe fifty dwellings and a few stores on lower Court street, seemed very picturesque and attractive. After forty years I have not changed my opinion. We found a suitable tract of prairie just across the line in Jefferson county, which we bought of the Burlington and Missouri River railroad at $3.50 per acre on easy payments. Beatrice remained our chief place of business. Smith Brothers had just started a banking business in one-half of a little shack, the other half being occupied by a watchmaker carrying a small stock of jewelry. Klein & Lang had a general store on the corner of Second and Court streets, and here we did nearly all of our trading. The "Pacific House" on Second street was the only hotel. Here I made headquarters for some time. Mr. and Mrs. Randall, the hosts, were very kind to me. The latter died a few years later in the prime of her life.

We soon commenced to build up what was for years known as "Jansen's Ranch," about twenty miles southwest of Beatrice, and stock it with sheep, which we brought from Wisconsin. The first summer I had a temporary sheep corral about where the West Side schoolhouse now stands. We used to drive from the ranch to Beatrice diagonally across the prairie; very few section lines had been established, and there was only one house between the two points.

Major Wheeler, of stage route fame, lived at the Pacific house and took a kindly interest in the young emigrant boy. I remember on one occasion I had brought in a carload of valuable breeding sheep and quartered them for the night in the corral of the livery stable across the street from the hotel, run then by S. P. Lester. I was afraid of strange dogs attacking them and sat up all night on the porch watching. In the morning, while washing up in the primitive wash-room, I overheard the major telling Mr. Randall about it. He concluded by saying: "That young fellow is all right; a boy who sits up all night with a few sheep will certainly succeed." I felt proud over the praise, and it encouraged me very much.

We were told by the few settlers who had preceded us that the upland prairie would not grow anything and that the bottom land was the only place where crops could be raised with any assurance of success. However, we were going to try farming, anyway. I bought a yoke of young oxen and a breaking plow and started in. The oxen were not well broken, and the plow was new and would not scour. Besides, I did not know anything about breaking prairie or driving oxen. The latter finally became impatient and ran away, dragging the plow with them. It was a hot day in May, and they headed for a nearby slough, going into the water up to their sides. I had by that time discarded my shoes and followed them as fast as I could. When I reached the slough, quite out of breath and thoroughly disgusted, I sat down and nearly cried and wished I were back in Russia where I did not have to drive oxen myself. About this time the nearest neighbor, a Mr. Babcock, living four miles away, happened along driving a team of old, well broken oxen. He asked what my trouble was, and after I told him in broken English, he said: "Well, Pete, take off your trousers and go in and get your oxen and plow out, and I will help you lay off the land and get your plow agoing," which he did, and so started me farming.

My younger brother, John, and I bached it for two years. One of us would herd the sheep and the other stay at home and do the chores and cooking. We took turns about every week. We had a room partitioned off in the end of the sheep shed, where we lived.

Game was plentiful those days, and during the fall and winter we never lacked for meat.

I had by that time, I regret to say, acquired the filthy American habit of chewing (I have quit it long since), and enjoyed it very much while doing the lonely stunt of herding the flock.

One day we had gotten a new supply of groceries and also a big plug of what was known as "Star" chewing tobacco. Next morning, I started out on my pony with the sheep, the plug in my pocket, and anticipating a good time. Soon a severe thunder storm came up, and lightning was striking all around me. I felt sure I would be hit, and they would find me dead with the big plug of tobacco in my pocket. My mother knew nothing of my bad habit, and I also knew that it would nearly kill her to find out, so I threw the plug far away and felt better—for awhile. The clouds soon passed away, however, and the sun came out brightly and soon found me hunting for that plug, which, to my great disappointment, I never recovered.

Those early winters, seems to me, were severer than they are now, and the snow storms or blizzards much fiercer, probably because the wind had an unrestricted sweep over the vast prairies.

In a few years, our flocks had increased, so that we built a corral and shed a mile and a half away, where we kept our band of wethers and a herder.

About Christmas, I think it was in 1880, a blizzard started, as they usually did, with a gentle fall of snow, which lasted the first day. During the night, the wind veered to the north, and in the morning, we could not see three rods; it seemed like a sea of milk!

We were very anxious to know the fate of our herder and his band of sheep, and towards noon I attempted to reach them, hitching a pair of horses to a sleigh and taking a man along. We soon got lost and drove around in a circle, blinded by the snow, for hours, my companion giving up and resigning himself to death. We probably would have both perished had it not been for the sagacity of my near horse, to which I finally gave the reins,
being benummed myself. He brought us home, and you may believe the barking of the shepherd dogs sounded very musical to me as we neared the barn.

We got our fuel from the Indian reservation about eight miles south of us on the creek, where now stands the thriving town of Diller. The Indians were not allowed to sell any timber, but a generous gift of tobacco was too tempting to them to resist.

Rattlesnakes were found frequently in those days, and their venomous bites caused great agony and sometimes death. One Sunday afternoon, wife and myself were sitting on the porch of our small frame house, while our baby was playing a few feet away in a pile of sand. Our attention was attracted by her loud and gleeful crooning. Looking up, we saw her poking a stick at a big rattler, coiled, ready to spring, about three feet away. I have always detested snakes and would give even a harmless bull-snake a wide berth. However, I took one big jump and landed on Mr. Rattler with both feet, while my wife snatched the baby out of harm's way.

The next ten years made a great change. We had proven that farming on the tablelands could be made a success, railroads had been built, and towns and villages had sprung up like mushrooms. We even got a telephone. The wilderness had been conquered.

When I look back upon those first years of early settlement, with their privations and hardships, I cannot refrain from thinking they were the happiest ones of my life, especially after I got married in 1877 and my dear wife came to share joy and sorrow with me. To her I attribute to a very large extent what little I may have achieved in the way of helping to build up this great commonwealth.

74

*The ancestors of Peter Jansen were among the first to embrace the
Mennonite faith in Prussia in the 16th century. To avoid religious
persecution and forced military service, the Jansens and 189 other
families moved to Russia in the 1870's. Descendants of these settlers,
including Cornelius Jansen, father of Peter, moved back to Germany
in late 1852 as the Crimean War approached, but returned to Russia
in 1856. Peter Jansen was born in Berdjansk, southern Russia on
March 21, 1852. As rumors of the introduction of general military
service grew around 1870, many Mennonites decided to leave Russia
and settle where conscription would not be an issue. As Cornelius
Jansen supported and organized emigration efforts, he was expelled
by the Russian government in 1873. After a brief stay in Berlin,
Ontario, Canada, the Jansens moved to America in 1874, first settling
in Iowa. A short time later, Peter Jansen purchased land in Jefferson
County, Nebraska. This is where the town of Jansen now stands.
Cornelius Jansen, called by many "the Moses of a great migration"
successfully encouraged other Mennonite families to purchase a vast
acreage from the Burlington and Missouri River Railroad. Peter
Jansen went into the sheep ranching business, feeding from 8,000 to
10,000 sheep a season and marketing as much as 200,000 pounds of*

wool. At one time, his herd ran as high as 25,000 head. Jansen was elected justice of the peace in 1880. A staunch Republican and supporter of the gold standard, he was an alternate to the Republican National Convention in 1884 and a delegate-at-large in 1896. He served in Nebraska Senate in 1911. Peter Jansen died in Beatrice, Nebraska, on June 6, 1923. He was survived by three daughters. His wife, Gertrude (Penner) Jansen, and son, John Jansen, preceded him in death.

Mr. Jansen wrote his full story in Memoirs of Peter Jansen, The Record of a Busy Life, An Autobiography *(Published by the author, Beatrice, Nebraska, 1921).*

EARLY RECOLLECTIONS OF GAGE COUNTY

BY MRS. E. JOHNSON

Emerson aptly said, "America is another word for opportunity." We realize this most truly when we compare present prosperity with early day living in the middle West.

In 1878 my brother, A. M. McMaster, and family, arrived in Nebraska City. They came overland to Gage county and settled on section 15, two and a half miles northeast of Filley and one mile south of what was then known as Melroy post office, so-called in honor of two little boys born the same year the post office was established, Mell Gale and Roy Tinklepaugh, whose parents were among the earliest settlers in this neighborhood.

My brother built his house of lumber he had shipped to Nebraska City. Beatrice was our marketplace. We sold all our grain, hogs, and produce there. Eggs were five cents a dozen and butter six cents a pound. The first year we came we bought five hundred bushels of corn at twelve cents a bushel delivered and cribbed it.

There was an Indian trail across the farm, and often the Indians would pass going from the Omaha reservation to the Otoe reservation at Barnston; the children would become frightened and hide under the bed; the Indians would often call and ask for flour and meat.

There was not a house between Elijah Filley's stone barn and Beatrice on the Scott street road, and no bridges. The trail we followed going to Beatrice led us north to Melroy, making the traveling distance one and a half miles farther than in these times of well-preserved section lines and graded country roads. This stone barn of Elijah Filley's was an early landmark. I have heard Mr. Filley tell interesting anecdotes of his early years here, one of an Indian battle near the present site of Virginia.

Before the town of Filley was in existence, there was a post office called "Cottage Hill," which is shown on old time maps of the state.

One of the curiosities of the early times was a cow with a wooden leg, running with a herd of cattle. The hind leg was off at the knee joint. She was furnishing milk for the family of her owner, a Mr. Scott living on Mud creek, near the town of Filley.

Mr. Scott often told of pounding their corn to pulverize it. The nearest mill was at Nebraska City. This difficult traffic continued until 1883, when the Burlington came through Filley.

Two or three years after we had located here, two young men came along from Kansas looking for work. My brother was away from home, working at carpentry, and his wife, fearing to be alone, would lock the stair door after they retired and unlock it in the morning before they appeared. They gathered the corn and then remained and worked for their board. One day, one of the young men was taken sick. The other was sent for Dr. Boggs. He lost his way in a raging blizzard and came out five miles north of where he intended to, but reached the doctor and secured medicine, the doctor not being able to go.

The next day Dr. Boggs, with his son to shovel through the drifts, succeeded in getting there. The young man grew worse, they sent for his mother, and she came by stage. The storm was so fierce the stage was left there for a week; the horses were taken to Melroy post office. The young man died and was taken in the stage to Beatrice to be shipped home, men going with shovels to dig a road. Arriving there it was found that the railroad was blocked. As they could not ship the body, they secured a casket and the next day brought it back to our house. My brother was not at home, and they took the corpse to a neighbor's house. The next day they buried him four miles east, at what is now known as Crab Orchard.

True, life in those days tended to make our people sturdy, independent and ingenious, but for real comfort it is not strange that we prefer present day living, with good mail service, easy modes of transportation, modern houses, and well equipped educational institutions.

A BUFFALO HUNT

BY W. H. AVERY

In the fall of 1866, about the last of October, a party of nine men, myself included, started out from Rose creek for a buffalo hunt. At Whiterock, Kansas, we were joined by another party of four men with "Old Martin Fisher," an early Whiterock settler, as official guide. Our equipment consisted of four wagons, one of which was drawn by a double ox team. There were numerous firearms and plenty of provisions for the trip. The party was much elated over the first day's experiences as night found us in possession of four fine buffalo.

That evening while we were riding out after one of the buffalo our ears were greeted by the Indian yell. Looking back up a draw we saw five redmen galloping toward us. At the time we did not know they were friendly, but that was proven later. They came up to us and wanted powder or "bullet" and also wanted to swap guns. All they succeeded in getting was a necktie which one of the men gave them. After a short parley among themselves they left, going back to our camp where we had left one man to guard the camp and prepare supper. There they helped themselves to the loaf of bread the guard had just baked, a $12 coat, a $22 revolver, and one good bridle; away they went and that was the last seen of them. The night was passed in safety and the next day we hunted without any exciting experiences.

The following day we met with only fair success so thought we had better start for home. In the morning, the party divided, our guide, Fisher, and two men going on and leaving the rest of us to hunt as we went along. We succeeded in getting only one buffalo, but Fisher's men had done better and were ready to make tracks for home. That night they had suspicions that there were Indians near so built no fire and in the morning soon after breaking camp a party of Indians came upon them.

There was considerable parleying about a number of things which the Indians wanted but the men were unwilling to make any bargains whatever. All the Indians but one started off and this one still wanted to parley and suddenly drew his revolver and shot Fisher in the shoulder. The Indian then rode off at breakneck speed and that was the last seen of them. Fisher warned the men not to shoot as he was uncertain as to how many redmen might be in their vicinity and he did not want to take any great risk of them all being killed. Our party did not know of the accident until we returned home, and we had no encounter with the party of Indians. We were thankful to be safely home after a ten days hunt.

A GRASSHOPPER RAID

BY EDNA M. BOYLE ALLEN

Perhaps children who live in a pioneer country remember incidents in their early life better than children living in older settled countries. These impressions stand out clearly and in prominence all the rest of their lives.

At least there are several things which happened before I was six years old that are as vivid in my memory as if they had happened but yesterday. Such was the coming of the grasshoppers in 1874, when I was two years old.

My father, Judge Boyle, then owned the block on the north side of Fifth street between I and J streets, in the village of Fairbury. Our house stood where J. A. Westling's house now stands. Near our place passed the stage road to Beatrice. A common remark then was, "We are almost to Fairbury, there is Boyle's house."

Father always had a big garden of sweet corn, tomatoes, cabbage, etc., and that year it was especially fine.

One day he came rushing home from his office saying, "The grasshoppers are coming." Mother and he hurried to the garden to save all the vegetables possible before the grasshoppers arrived. I put on a little pink sunbonnet of which I was very proud, and went out to watch my parents gather the garden truck as fast as they could and run to the cellar door and toss it down. I jumped up and down thoroughly enjoying the excitement.

Finally, the grasshoppers, which were coming from the northwest like a dark cloud, seeming so close, father shut the cellar door before he and mother returned to the garden for another load. They had just filled their arms when the grasshoppers began to drop and not wishing to let any down cellar, they threw what vegetables they had on the ground and turned a big wooden wash tub over them. By this time, my little pink sunbonnet was covered with big grasshoppers. Mother picked me up in her arms and we hurried into the house. From the north kitchen window, we watched every stalk of that garden disappear, even the onions were eaten from the ground.

When father went to get the vegetables from under the wooden tub there wasn't a thing there. The grasshoppers had managed to crawl and dig their way under the edge of that tub.

The only time an Indian ever frightened me was in the fall of 1875. I was used to having the Otoe Indians come to our house. Mother was not afraid of them so of course I was not. Among them was a big fellow called John Little Pipe. The door in the hall of our house had glass in the upper half. One afternoon mother being nearly sick was lying down on the couch and I took my doll trying to keep quiet playing in the hall. Looking up suddenly I saw John stooping and looking in through the glass in the door. I screamed and ran to mother. He didn't like my screaming but followed me into the sitting room and upon seeing mother lying down said, "White lady sick?" Mother was on her feet in a moment.

He sat down and after grumbling a while about my screaming he began to beg for a suit of clothes. Mother said, "John, you know well enough you are too large to wear my husband's clothes." Then he wanted something for his squaw and children. Finally, mother gave him an old dress of hers. He looked it over critically and asked for goods to patch it where it was worn thin. Grabbing his blanket where it lay across his knees, he shook it saying, "Wind, whew, whew." After receiving the patches, he wanted food, but mother told him he could not have a thing more and for him to go. He started, but toward the closet he had seen her take the dress from. She said, "You know better than to go to that door. You go out the way you came in." He meekly obeyed. I had seen him many times before and saw him several times afterward but that was the only time I was frightened.

Albert Lamborn Green (1845-1947), a Quaker, was appointed as the Indian agent for the Oto tribe by President Ulysses S. Grant in 1869. He wrote and illustrated an account of his experiences that is one of the earliest sources documenting the Oto way of life. The account includes a small dictionary of useful words in the Oto language. Though his term as agent ended in 1872, when he moved to the young town of Beatrice, Nebraska, Green maintained friendships with the Otoes throughout his life.

Green also wrote and illustrated numerous poems and stories for his children and grandchildren. Though humorous and whimsical, they usually contained a lesson or ended with a moral. "Peter Pike's Reformation," seen here, is Green's retelling of the "Grasshopper and the Ant" fable. Peter learns a lesson about laziness and diligence when he dreams he has been transformed into an ant -- or is it a dream?[8]

---

[8] https://history.nebraska.gov/blog/albert-lamborn-green-drawings

EARLY DAYS IN PAWNEE COUNTY

BY DANIEL B. CROPSEY

In March 1868, I left Fairbury, Illinois, with my two brothers and a boy friend in a covered wagon drawn by two mules. We landed at Nebraska City after swimming the mules to get to the ferry on which we crossed the Big Muddy. We then drove to Lincoln the first week in April. My father had purchased a home there on the site where the Capital hotel now stands. Lincoln then was but a hamlet of a few hundred people. There were no shade trees nor sidewalks and no railroad. Later father built a larger house, out a considerable distance in those days, but today it faces the capitol building. The house is a brick structure, and all the bricks were hauled from Nebraska City. Afterwards father sold the home to Chancellor Fairfield of the State University.

The year before we came father had come to Nebraska and had bought a large body of land, about ten thousand acres, in Pawnee county. I being the oldest boy in our family, it devolved upon me to go to Pawnee county to look after the land, which was upland and considered by the older inhabitants of little value; but the tract is now worth about a million dollars. Among other duties I superintended the opening up of the lines and plowing out fifty-two miles of hedge rows around and through this land. I am sorry

85

to say that most of the money and labor were lost for prairie fires almost completely destroyed the hedge.

I had many experiences during my two years' sojourn in Pawnee county. The work was hard and tedious. Shelter and drinking-water were scarce—we drank water from the buffalo wallows or went thirsty, and at times had to brave the storms in the open. The people were poor, and many lived in sod houses or "dugouts," and the living was very plain. Meat and fruit were rarities. The good people I lived with did their best to provide, but they were up against it. Grasshoppers and the drouth were things they had to contend with. At times, our meals consisted of bread and butter and pumpkin, with pumpkin pie for Sunday dinner. The barn we usually carried with us. It consisted of a rope from sixty to a hundred feet long for each mule or horse and was called the lariat. I put the pony one night in the barn across the ravine, I well remember, and in the morning, I found a river between the barn and me. A rain had fallen in the night and I had to wait nearly a day before I could get to the pony.

Our only amusement was running down young deer and rabbits and killing rattlesnakes.

We often met the red man with his paint and feathers. He was ever ready to greet you with "How!" and also ready to trade ponies, and never backward about asking for "tobac." As I was neither brave nor well acquainted with the Indians, I was always ready to divide my "tobac." Later I found out I was easy, for the boys told me whenever they met the beggar Indian, they told him to "puckachee," which they said meant for him to move on.

We had no banks, and we cashed our drafts with the merchants. David Butler was governor at that time. He was a merchant as well, and made his home in Pawnee, so he was my banker. On two occasions I had the pleasure of riding with him in his buggy from Pawnee to Lincoln. It was indeed a privilege to ride in a buggy, for we all rode ponies those days, and I think I was envied by most of the boys and girls of Pawnee.

On one of my return trips with the governor my good mother had baked a nice cake for me to take with me, which I put under the seat along with a lot of wines of several kinds and grades which the governor's friends had given him. Of course, mother didn't know about the liquids. I'll never forget that trip. We grew very sociable and the Nemaha valley grew wider and wider as we drove along; and when we arrived at Pawnee the next day the cake was all gone, our faces were like full moons, and it was fully a week before I had any feeling in my flesh.

I also well remember the first train which ran between Lincoln and Plattsmouth. That was a great day, and the Burlington excursion was made up of box cars and flat cars with ties for seats. Crowds of young people took advantage of the excursion and we enjoyed it much more than we would today in a well-equipped pullman.

Daniel B. Cropsey, Representative from the Thirty-sixth District, composed of Thayer and Jefferson counties, was born in Ohio, October 12, 1848. He received a thorough education in the schools of his native state and of Illinois. In 1868 he removed from Fairbury, Illinois, to Lincoln, Nebraska. He served two terms as city treasurer of Lincoln and in 1882 became a resident of

Fairbury, Nebraska, his present home. There he engaged in the banking business, and at the present time is the president of the First National Bank of Fairbury, Nebraska, and also president of the National Bank of Wilber, Nebraska, and the Exchange Bank of Steele City, Nebraska. He is a member of the Masonic Lodge of Fairbury and has served as mayor of that city.

The father of Representative Cropsey was a colonel in the Union Army during the Civil War and served as a member of the Illinois Legislature and later was a member of the Nebraska State Senate. Representative Cropsey was married in 1873 to Miss Myra Caldwell, and has one child, a daughter. Mr. Cropsey is serving as chairman of the House Committee on Insurance.[9]

---

[9] 1903 -
http://www.usgennet.org/usa/ne/topic/resources/OLLibrary/Legislature/1903/pages/nelg0079.htm

THE EARLIEST ROMANCE OF JEFFERSON COUNTY, NEBRASKA

BY GEORGE W. HANSEN

One hundred and three years ago Hannah Norton was born "away down east" in the state of Maine. Hannah married Jason Plummer, and in the year 1844, seized by the wanderlust, they decided to move west. One morning their little daughter Eleanor, four years old, stood outside the cabin door with her rag doll pressed tightly to her breast, and watched her parents load their household goods into the heavy, covered wagon, yoke up the oxen, and make preparations for a long journey.

As little Eleanor clambered up the wheel and into the wagon, she felt none of the responsibilities of the long pioneer life that lay before her, nor did she know or care about her glorious ancestry.

Only a few decades previous her ancestor, Major Peter Norton, who had fought gallantly in the war of the Revolution, had gone to his reward. His recompense on earth had been the consciousness of patriotic duty well performed in the cause of liberty and independence. A hero he was, but the Maine woods were full of Revolutionary heroes. He was not yet famous. It was reserved for

89

Peter Norton's great-great-great-granddaughters to perpetuate the story of his heroic deeds. One, Mrs. Auta Helvey Pursell, the daughter of our little Eleanor, is now a member of Quivera chapter, D. A. R., of Fairbury, Nebraska, and another, Lillian Norton, is better known to the world she has charmed with her song, as Madame Nordica.

But little Eleanor was wholly unmindful of past or future on that morning long ago. She laughed and chattered as the wagon rolled slowly on its westward way.

A long, slow, and painful journey through forests and over mountains, then down the Ohio river to Cincinnati was at last finished, and the family made that city their home. After several years, the oxen were again yoked up and the family traveled to the West, out to the prairies of Iowa, where they remained until 1863. Then, hearing of a still fairer country where free homes could be taken in fertile valleys that needed no clearing, where wild game was abundant and chills and fever unknown, Jason, Hannah, and Eleanor again traveled westward. After a toilsome journey they settled in Swan creek valley, Nebraska territory, near the present northern line of Jefferson county.

Theirs were pioneer surroundings. The only residents were ranchers scattered along the creeks at the crossings of the Oregon trail. A few immigrants came that year and settled in the valleys of the Sandys, Swan creek, Cub creek, Rose creek, and the Little Blue. No human habitation stood upon the upland prairies. The population was four-fifths male, and the young men traveled up and down the creeks for miles seeking partners for their dances, which were often given. But it was always necessary for a number of men to take the part of ladies. In such cases they wore a handkerchief around one arm to distinguish them.

The advent of a new family into the country was an important event, and especially when a beautiful young lady formed a part of it. The families of Joel Helvey and Jason Plummer became neighborly at once, visiting back and forth with the friendly intimacy characteristic of all pioneers. Paths were soon worn over the divide between Joel Helvey's ranch on the Little Sandy and the Plummer home on Swan creek, and one of Joel's boys was accused of making clandestine rambles in that direction. Certain it was that many of the young men who asked Eleanor for her company to the dances were invariably told that Frank Helvey had already spoken. Their dejection was explained in the vernacular of the time—they had "gotten the mitten."

The music for the dances was furnished by the most energetic fiddlers in the land, and the art of playing "Fisher's Hornpipe," "Devil's Dream," and "Arkansaw Traveler" in such lively, triumphant tones of the fiddle as played by Joe Baker and Hiram Helvey has been lost to the world. Sometimes disputes were settled either before or after the dance by an old-fashioned fist fight. In those days, the accepted policy was that if you threshed your adversary soundly, the controversy was settled—there was no further argument about it. At one dance on the Little Sandy some "boys" from the Blue decided to "clear out" the ranchers before the dance, and in the lively melee that followed, Frank Helvey inadvertently got his thumb in his adversary's mouth; and he will show you yet a scar and cloven nail to prove this story. The ranchers more than held their own, and after the battle invited the defeated party to take part in the dance. The invitation was accepted and, in the morning, all parted good friends.

On August 6, 1864, the Overland stage, which had been turned back on its way to the west, brought news that the Sioux and Cheyenne were on the warpath. They had massacred entire settlements on the Little Blue and along the trail a few miles west and were planning to kill every white person west of Beatrice and Marysville.

For some time, the friendly old Indians had told Joel Helvey that the young men were chanting the old song:

"Some day we shall drive the whites back
Across the great salt water
Whence they came;

Happy days for the Sioux
When the whites go back."

Little attention had been paid to these warnings, the Helvey family believing they could take care of themselves as they had during the past eighteen years in the Indian country. But the report brought by the stage was too alarming to be disregarded; and the women asked to be taken to a place of safety.

At this time Mrs. Plummer and her daughter Eleanor were visiting at the home of Joel Helvey. They could not return to Swan creek, for news had come that all Swan creek settlers had gone to Beatrice. There was no time to be lost. The women and father Helvey, who was then in failing health, were placed in wagons, the boys mounted horses to drive the cattle, and all "struck out" over the trail following the divide towards Marysville, where breastworks had been thrown up and stockades had been built.

During the day Frank found many excuses to leave the cattle with his brothers while he rode close to the wagon in which Eleanor was seated. It was a time to try one's courage and he beguiled the anxious hours with tales of greater dangers than the impending one and assured her, with many a vow of love, that he could protect her from any attack the Indians might make.

The first night the party camped at the waterhole two miles northwest of the place where now an imposing monument marks the crossing of the Oregon trail and the Nebraska-Kansas line. Towards evening of the next day, they halted on Horseshoe creek. In the morning it was decided to make this their permanent camp. There was abundant grass for their stock, and here they would cut and stack their winter hay.

A man in the distance saw the camp and ponies, and mistaking the party for Indians, hurried to Marysville and gave the alarm. Captain Hollenberg and a squad of militia came out and from a safe distance investigated with a spyglass. Finding the party were white people he came down and ordered them into Marysville. The captain said the Indians would kill them all and, inflamed by the bloodshed, would be more ferocious in their attack on the stockade.

The Helveys preferred taking their chances with the Indians rather than leave their cattle to the mercies of the Kansas Jayhawkers, and told the captain that when the Indians came, they would get to Marysville first and give the alarm.

Their camp was an ideal spot under the grateful shadow of noble trees. The songs of birds in the branches above them, the odor of prairie flowers and the new-mown hay about them, lent charm to the scene. Two of the party, at least, lived in an enchanted land. After the blistering heat of an August day Frank and Eleanor walked together in the shadows and coolness of night and watched the moon rise through the trees. And here was told the old, old story, world old yet ever new. Here were laid the happy plans for future years. And yet through all these happy days there ran a thread of sorrow. Father Joel Helvey failed rapidly, and on September 3 he passed away. After he was laid to rest, the entire party returned to the ranch on Little Sandy.

The day for the wedding, September 21, at last arrived. None of the officers qualified to perform marriage ceremonies having returned since the Indian raid, Frank and Eleanor, with Frank's sister as chaperon, drove to Beatrice. On arriving there they were delighted to meet Eleanor's father. His consent to the marriage was obtained and he was asked to give away the bride. The marriage party proceeded to Judge Towle's cabin on the Big Blue where the wedding ceremony was solemnly performed and "Pap" Towle gave the bride the first kiss.

And thus, just fifty years ago, the first courtship in Jefferson county was consummated.

EXPERIENCES ON THE FRONTIER

BY FRANK HELVEY

I was born July 7, 1841, in Huntington county, Indiana. My father, Joel Helvey, decided in 1846 to try his fortune in the far West. Our family consisted of father, mother, three boys, and three girls. So, two heavy wagons were fitted up to haul heavy goods, and a light wagon for mother and the girls. The wagons were the old-fashioned type, built very heavy, carrying the customary tar bucket on the rear axle.

Nebraska was at this time in what was called the Indian country, and no one was allowed to settle in it. We stopped at old Fort Kearny—now Nebraska City. In a short time, we pulled up stakes and housed in a log cabin on the Iowa side. Father, two brothers—Thomas and Whitman—and I constructed a ferry to run across the Missouri river, getting consent of the commandant at the fort to move the family over on the Nebraska side; but he said we would have to take our chances with the Indians. We broke a small patch of ground, planting pumpkins, melons, corn, etc. The Indians were very glad to see us and very friendly—in fact, too much so. When our corn and melons began to ripen, they would come in small bands, gather the corn, and fill their blankets. It did no good for us to protest, so we boys thought we would scare them away. We hid in the bushes close to the field. Soon they came and were

94

filling their blankets. We shot over their heads, but the Indians didn't scare—they came running straight toward us. They gave us a little of our own medicine and took a few shots at us. We didn't scare any more Indians.

When word came in the fall of 1858 that gold had been discovered in Pike's Peak by the wagonload, that settled it. We got the fever, and in April 1859, we started for Pike's Peak. We went by the way of Beatrice, striking the Overland trail near the Big Sandy. An ex-soldier, Tim Taylor, told us he believed the Little Sandy to be the best place in southern Nebraska. We built a ranch house on the trail at the crossing of Little Sandy and engaged in freighting from the Missouri river to the Rocky Mountains. This we did for several years, receiving seven to eight cents per pound. We hauled seven thousand to eight thousand pounds on a wagon, and it required from seventy-five to eighty days to make a round trip with eight and ten yoke of oxen to a wagon. I spent about nine years freighting across the plains from Atchison, Leavenworth, St. Joseph, and Nebraska City to Denver, hauling government supplies to Fort Laramie. In 1863-64 I served as substitute stage driver, messenger, or pony express rider. I have met at some time or another nearly every noted character or "bad man" that passed up and down the trail. I met Wild Bill for the first time at Rock Creek ranch. I met him often after the killing of McCanles and helped bury the dead. I was well acquainted with McCanles. Wild Bill was a remarkable man, unexcelled as a shot, hard to get acquainted with. Lyman, or Jack, Slade was considered the worst man-killer on the plains.

The Indians did not give us much trouble until the closing year of the civil war. Our trains were held up several times, being forced to corral. We were fortunate not to lose a man. I have shot at hundreds of Indians. I cannot say positively that I ever killed one, although I was considered a crack shot. I can remember of twenty or more staying with us one night, stretching out on their blankets before the fireplace, and departing in the morning without making a move out of the way. The Pawnees and Otoes were very bitter toward the Sioux and Cheyennes. In the summer of 1862 over five hundred Indians were engaged in an all-day fight on the Little Blue river south of Meridian. That night over a hundred warriors danced around a camp-fire with the scalps of their foes on a pole, catching the bloody scalp with their teeth. How many were killed we never knew.

My brothers and I went on one special buffalo hunt with three different tribes of Indians—Otoes, Omahas, and Pawnees—about one thousand in all, on Rose creek, about where the town of Hubbell is situated. We were gone about four days. The Indians would do all the killing. When they got what they wanted, then we boys would get our meat. There was plenty for all. The prairies were covered with buffalo; they were never out of sight. On the 4th of July 1859, six of us with two wagons, four yoke of oxen to a wagon, went over on the Republican where there were always thousands of buffalo. We were out two weeks and killed what meat we wanted. We always had a guard out at night when we camped, keeping the wolves from our fresh meat. We came home to the ranch heavily loaded. We sold some and dried some for our own use.

I homesteaded, June 13, 1866, on the Little Blue, five miles northwest of Fairbury, and helped the settlers looking for homesteads locate their land. My father, Joel Helvey, entered forty acres where we had established our ranch on Little Sandy in 1861, the first year any land was entered in this county. I was the first sheriff of this county; served four years, 1867-1870. No sheriff had qualified or served before 1867. County business was done at Big Sandy and Meridian, and at the houses of the county officers. We carried the county records around from place to place in gunny sacks.

I am glad I participated in the earliest happenings of this county and am proud to be one of its citizens.

Benjamin Franklin Helvey

Benjamin Franklin Helvey burial site in Fairbury Cemetery, Jefferson County, Nebraska

LOOKING BACKWARD

BY GEORGE E. JENKINS

Looking backward forty years and more, I feel as Longfellow so beautifully expresses it,

"You may build more splendid habitations,
Fill your rooms with sculpture and with paintings,
But you cannot buy with gold the old associations,"

for in that time I have seen Fairbury grow from a little hamlet to a city of the first class, surrounded by a country that we used to call "the Indian country," considered unfit for agricultural purposes, but today it blossoms as the rose and no finer land lies anywhere.

I have read with great interest of the happenings of ten, twenty, thirty years ago as published each week in our Fairbury papers, but am going to delve into ancient history a little deeper and tell you from personal experience of the interesting picture presented to me forty-odd years ago, I think in the year 70 or '71, for I distinctly remember the day I caught the first glimpse of Fairbury. It was a bright and sunshiny morning in July. We had been making the towns in western Kansas and had gotten rather a late start from Concordia the day before; a storm coming up suddenly compelled us to seek shelter for the night. My traveling companion was A. V. Whiting, selling shoes, and I was selling dry-goods, both from wholesale houses in St. Joseph, Missouri. Mr. Whiting is well and honorably known in Fairbury as he was afterwards in business there for many years. He has been a resident of Lincoln for twenty-three years.

There were no railroads or automobiles in the country at that time and we had to depend on a good pair of horses and a covered spring wagon. We found a place of shelter at Marks' mill, located on Rose creek fifteen miles southwest of Fairbury, and here we stayed all night. I shall always remember our introduction there, viz: as we drove up to the house I saw a large, portly old man coming in from the field on top of a load of hay, and as I approached him I said, "My name is Jenkins, sir—" but before I could say more he answered in a deep bass voice, saying, "My name is Clodhopper, sir," which he afterwards explained was the name that preachers of the United Brethren church were known by at that time. This man, Marks, was one of the first county treasurers of Jefferson county, and it is related of him that while he was treasurer he had occasion to go to Lincoln, the capital of the state, to pay the taxes of the county, and being on horseback he lost his way and meeting a horseman with a gun across his shoulder, he said to the stranger, "I am treasurer of Jefferson county. My saddle-bags are full of gold and I am on the way to Lincoln to pay the taxes of the county, but I have lost my way. Please direct me."

Returning to my story of stopping over night at Rose creek: we were most hospitably entertained and at breakfast next morning we were greatly surprised on being asked if we would have wild or tame sweetening in our coffee, as this was the first time in all our travels we had ever been asked that question. We were told that honey was wild sweetening and sugar the tame sweetening.

I cannot refrain from telling a little incident that occurred at this time. When we had our team hitched up and our sample trunks aboard, we asked Mr. Marks for our bill and were told we could not pay anything for our entertainment, and just then Mrs. Marks appeared on the scene. She had in her hand a lot of five and ten cent war shinplasters, and as she handed them to Mr. Marks he said, "Mother and I have been talking the matter over and as we have not bought any goods from you we decided to give you a dollar to help you pay expenses elsewhere"; and on our refusing to take it he said, "I want you to take it, for it is worth it for the example you have set to my children." Politely declining the money and thanking our host and hostess for their good opinion and splendid entertainment, we were soon on our way to pay our first visit to Fairbury.

We arrived about noon and stopped at a little one-story hotel on the west side of the square, kept by a man by the name of Hurd. After dinner we went out to see the town and were told it was the county-seat of Jefferson county. The courthouse was a little one-story frame building and is now located on the west side of the square and known as Christian's candy shop. There was one large general store kept by Champlin & McDowell, a drug store, a hardware store, lumber yard, blacksmith shop, a schoolhouse, church, and a few small buildings scattered around the square. The residences were small and widely scattered. Primitive conditions prevailed everywhere, and we were told the population was one hundred and fifty, but we doubted it. The old adage reads, "Big oaks from little acorns grow," and it has been my privilege and great pleasure to have seen Fairbury "climb the ladder round by round" until today it has a population of fifty-five hundred.

THE EASTER STORM OF 1873

BY CHARLES B. LETTON

Spring opened very early in the year 1873. Farmers plowed and harrowed the ground and sowed their oats and spring wheat in February and March. The grass began to grow early in April and by the middle of the month the small-grain fields were bright green with the new crops. Most of the settlers on the uplands of Jefferson county were still living in dugouts or sod houses. The stables and barns for the protection of their live stock were for the most part built by setting forked posts in the ground, putting rough poles and brush against the sides and on the roof, and covering them with straw, prairie grass, or manure. Sometimes the bank of a ravine was made perpendicular and used as one side. The covering of the walls and roof of these structures needed continual renewal as the winds loosened it or as the spring rains caused it to settle. Settlers became careless about this early in the spring, thinking that the winter was over. The prairies were still bare of hedges, fences, or trees to break the winds or catch the drifting snow.

Easter Sunday occurred on the thirteenth of April. For days before, the weather had been mild and the air delightful. The writer was then living alone in a dugout seven miles north of Fairbury in what is now the rich and fertile farming community known as Bower. The granary stood on the edge of a ravine a short distance from the dugout. The stable or barn was partly dug into the bank of this ravine; the long side was to the north, while the roof and the south side were built of poles and straw in the usual fashion of those days. On the afternoon of Easter Sunday, it began to rain and blow from the northwest. The next morning, I had been awake for some time waiting for daylight when I finally realized that the dim light coming from the windows was due to the fact that they were covered with snow drifts. I could hear the noise of the wind but had no idea of the fury of the tempest until I undertook to go outside to feed the stock. As soon as I opened the door, I found that the air was full of snow, driven by a tremendous gale from the north. The fury of the tempest was indescribable. The air appeared to be a mass of moving snow, and the wind howled like a pack of furies. I managed to get to the granary for some oats, but on looking into the ravine no stable was to be seen, only an immense snow drift which almost filled it. At the point where the door to the stable should have been there appeared a hole in the drift where the snow was eddying. On crawling into this I found that during the night the snow had drifted in around the horses and cattle, which were tied to the manger. The animals had trampled it under their feet to such an extent that it had raised them so that in places their backs lifted the flimsy roof, and the wind carrying much of the covering away, had filled the stable with snow until some of them were almost and others wholly buried, except where the remains of the roof protected them.

Two animals died while I was trying to extricate them and at night I was compelled to lead two or three others into the front room of the dugout and keep them there until the storm was over in order to save their lives. It was only by the most strenuous efforts I was able to get to the house. My clothing was stiff. The wind had driven the snow into the fabric, as it had thawed it had frozen again, until it formed an external coating of ice.

I had nothing to eat all day, having gone out before breakfast, and when night came and I attempted to build a fire in the cook stove I found that the storm had blown away the joints of stovepipe which projected through the roof and had drifted the hole so full of snow that the snow was in the stove itself. I went on the roof, cleared it out, built a fire, made some coffee and warmed some food, then went to bed utterly fatigued and, restlessly tossing, dreamed all night that I was still in the snow drift working as I had worked all day.

Many other settlers took their cattle and horses into their houses or dugouts in order to save them. Every ravine and hollow that ran in an easterly or westerly direction was filled with snow from rim to rim. In other localities cattle were driven many miles by this storm. Houses, or rather shacks, were unroofed and people in them frozen to death. Travelers caught in the blizzard, who attempted to take refuge in ravines, perished and their stiffened bodies were found when the drifts melted weeks afterward. Stories were told of people who had undertaken to go from their houses to their outbuildings and who, being blinded by the snow, became lost and either perished or nearly lost their lives, and of others where the settler in order to reach his well or his outbuildings in safety fastened a rope to the door and went into the storm holding to the rope in order to insure his safe return. Deer, antelope, and other wild animals perished in the more sparsely settled districts. The storm lasted for three days, not always of the same intensity, and freezing weather followed for a day or two thereafter. In a few days the sun shone, the snow melted, and spring reappeared; the melting drifts that lay for weeks in some places being the only reminder of the severity of the storm.

To old settlers in Nebraska and northern Kansas this has ever since been known as "The Easter Storm." In the forty-six years that I have lived in Nebraska there has only been one other winter storm that measurably approached it in intensity. This was the blizzard of 1888 when several people lost their lives. At that time, however, people were living in comfort; trees, hedges, groves, stubble, and cornfields held the snow so that the drifts were insignificant in comparison. The cold was more severe, but the duration of the storm was less, and no such widespread suffering took place.

EARLY EXPERIENCES IN NEBRASKA

BY ELIZABETH PORTER SEYMOUR

In the spring of 1872, we came from Waterloo, Iowa, to Plymouth, Nebraska. My husband drove through, and upon his arrival I came by train with my young brother and baby daughter four months old.

When my husband came the previous fall to buy land, there was no railroad south of Crete, and he drove across the country, but the railroad had since been completed to Beatrice. There was a mixed train, with one coach, and I was the only lady passenger. There was one young girl, who could not speak any English, but who had a card hung on her neck telling where she was to go. The trainmen held a consultation and decided that the people lived a short distance from the track, in the vicinity of Wilber, so they stopped the train and made inquiries. Finding these people expected someone, we waited until they came and got the girl. My husband met me at Beatrice, and the next morning we started on a fourteen-mile drive to Plymouth, perched upon a load of necessaries and baggage.

We had bought out a homesteader, so we had a shelter to go into. This consisted of a cottonwood house fourteen by sixteen feet, unplastered, and with a floor of rough boards. It was a dreary place, but in a few days, I had transformed it. One carpet was put on the floor and another stretched overhead on the joists. This made a place to store things and gave the room a better appearance. Around the sides of the room were tacked sheets, etc., making a white wall. On this we hung a few pictures, and when the homesteader appeared at the door, he stood amazed at our fine appearance. A rude lean-to was built to hold the kitchen stove and work-table.

Many times that summer a feeling of intense loneliness at the dreary condition came over me, but the baby Helen, always happy and smiling, drove gloom away. Then, in August, came the terrible blow of losing our baby blossom. Cholera infantum was the complaint. A young mother's ignorance of remedies, and the long distance from a doctor, caused a delay that was fatal.

Before we came, the settlers had built a log schoolhouse, with sod roof and plank seats. In the spring of 1872, the Congregational Home Missionary Society sent Rev. Henry Bates of Illinois to the field, and he organized a Congregational church of about twenty-five members, my husband and myself being charter members. For a time, we had service in the log schoolhouse, but soon had a comfortable building for services.

Most of the land about Plymouth was owned by a railroad company, and they laid out a townsite, put up a two-story schoolhouse, and promised a railroad soon. After years of waiting, the railroad came, but the station was about two miles north. Business went with the railroad to the new town, and the distinction was made between New Plymouth and Old Plymouth.

Prairie chickens and quail were quite abundant during the first years, and buffalo meat could often be bought, being shipped from the western part of the state. In the droves of cattle driven past our house to the Beatrice market, I have occasionally seen a buffalo.

Deer and wolves were sometimes seen, and coyotes often made havoc with our fowls, digging through the sod chicken house to rob the roosts. Rattlesnakes were frequently killed and much dreaded, but deaths from the bite were very rare, though serious illness often resulted.

Prairie fires caused the greatest terror, and the yearly losses were large. Everyone plowed fire guards and tried to be prepared, but, with tall grass and weeds and a strong wind, fire would be carried long distances and sweep everything before it with great rapidity.

Indians frequently camped on Cub creek for a few days in their journey from one reservation to another to visit. They would come to the houses to beg for food, and, though they never harmed us, we were afraid of them. More than once I have heard a slight noise in my kitchen, and on going out, found Indians in possession; they never knocked. I was glad to give them food and hasten their departure.

In the summer of 1873, quite a party of us went to the Otoe reservation to see just how the Indians lived. We had two covered wagons and one provision wagon. We cooked our food by a camp-fire, slept out of doors, and had a jolly time. We spent nearly one day on the reservation, visiting the agent's house and the school and peering into the huts of the Indians. At the schoolhouse, the pupils were studious, but several of them had to care for papooses while studying, and the Indians were peering into the doors and windows, watching proceedings. Most of the Indians wore only a blanket and breech cloth, but the teacher was evidently trying to induce the young pupils to wear clothes and succeeded in a degree. One boy amused us very much by wearing flour sacks for trousers. The sacks were simply ripped open at the end, the stamps of the brand being still upon them, one sack being lettered in red and the other in blue. Preparations were going on for a visit to the Omahas by a number of braves and some squaws, and they were donning paint and feathers. The agent had received some boxes of clothing from the East for them, which they were eager to wear on their trip. Not having enough to fit them out, one garment was given to each, and they at once put them on. It was very ludicrous to see them, one with a hat, another with a shirt, another with a vest, etc.

106

At last they were ready and rode away on their ponies. As we drove away, an Indian and squaw, with papoose, were just ahead of us. A thunder storm came up, and the brave Indian took away from the squaw her parasol and held it over his head, leaving her unprotected.

Although the settlers on the upland were widely scattered, they were kind and neighborly, as a rule—ready to help each other in all ways, especially in sickness and death. One Thanksgiving a large number of settlers brought their dinners to the church, and after morning services enjoyed a good dinner and social hour together. That church, so important a factor in the community in early days, was disbanded but a few years ago. Pioneer life has many privations, but there are also very many pleasant experiences.

LINCOLN IN THE EARLY SEVENTIES

BY (MRS. O. C.) MINNIE DEETTE POLLEY BELL

In the spring of 1874 my father, Hiram Polley, came from Ohio to Lincoln, I being a young lady of nineteen years. To say that the new country with its vast prairies, so different from our beautiful timber country, produced homesickness, would be putting it mildly. My parents went on to a farm near what is now the town of Raymond, I remaining in Lincoln with an aunt, Mrs. Watie E. Gosper. My father built the barn as soon as possible and this was used for the house until after the crops were put in, then work was begun on the house that they might have it before cold weather.

The first trouble that came was the devastating plague of grasshoppers which swept over this section of the country in the years 1874 and 1875. Not long after this a new trouble was upon us. The day dawned bright and fair, became hotter and more still, until presently in the distance there could be seen the effects of a slight breeze; this however was only the advance of a terrible windstorm. When the hurricane had passed, the barn, which only a few months before had served as the house, was in ruins. Undaunted, my father set about to rebuild the barn, which still remains on the farm; the farm, however, is now owned by other parties.

In the winter of 1875, there was quite a fall of snow, and one of the funny sights was a man driving down O street with a horse hitched to a rocking chair. Everything that could be used for a sleigh was pressed into service. This was a strange sight to me, having come from Ohio where we had from three to four months of sleighing with beautiful sleighs and all that goes to make up a merry time.

During this winter many were using corn for fuel and great quantities were piled on the ground, which of course made rats very plentiful—so much so that when walking on the streets at dusk one would almost have to kick them out of the way or wait for them to pass.

In the course of time a young man appeared upon the scene, and on December 10, 1874, I was married to Ortha C. Bell. We were married in the house which now stands at the northeast corner of Twelfth and M streets, then the home of my aunt, Mrs. Gosper. Four children were born to us: the first, a daughter, dying in infancy; the second, Jennie Bell-Ringer, of Lincoln; the third, a son, Ray Hiram Bell, dying at the age of three; and the fourth, a daughter, Hazel Bell-Smith. Two grandchildren have come to brighten our lives, DeEtte Bell Smith and Edmund Burke Smith. Our home at 931 D street, which we built in 1886, is still occupied by us.

Minnie DeEtte Polley was born October 25, 1854 and died March 4, 1942 at the age of 87. She was the daughter of Hiram Polley and Abigail Cooper.

Minnie spent her early days in Herkimer County, NY subsequently moving with her parents to Chagrin Falls, OH. She then moved to Lincoln with her parents in 1874 at the age of 19.

She was the wife of Ortha C. Bell. They were married December 10, 1874 in the house that still stands at the northeast corner of Twelfth and M Streets, then the home of Minnie's Aunt, Mrs. Gosper. Minnie and Ortha celebrated their Golden Wedding in 1924.[10]

GRAY EAGLE, PAWNEE CHIEF

BY MILLARD S. BINNEY

It is not often that one sees a real Indian chief on the streets of Fullerton, but such happened in June, 1913, when the city was visited by David Gillingham, as he is known in the English tongue, or Gray Eagle, as his people call him, chief of the Pawnees.

Gray Eagle is the son of White Eagle, whom the early inhabitants of Nance county will remember as chief of the Pawnees at the time the county was owned by that tribe.

Gray Eagle was born about three miles this side of Genoa, in 1861. He spent his boyhood in the county and when white men began to build at the place that is now Genoa, he attended school there. When he was fourteen years of age, he accompanied his tribe to its new home at Pawnee City, Oklahoma, where he has since resided. The trip overland was made mostly on horseback, and the memories of it are very interesting as interpreted to us by Chief Gray Eagle, and John Williamson, of Genoa, one of the few white men to make this long journey with the red men. Gray Eagle made one trip back here in 1879, visiting the spot that is now Fullerton—then only a few rude shacks.

Uppermost in Gray Eagle's mind had always been the desire to return and see what changes civilization had brought. In 1913 he

111

was sent to St. Louis as a delegate to the Baptist convention, after which he decided to visit the old scenes. From St. Louis he went to Chicago and from that city he came to Genoa.

"I have always wanted to see if I could locate the exact spot of my birth," said Gray Eagle, in perfect English, as he talked to us on this last visit, "and I have been successful in my undertaking. I found it last week, three miles this side of Genoa. I was born in a little, round mud-house, and although the house is long since gone, I discovered the circular mound that had been its foundation. I stood upon the very spot where I was born, and as I looked out over the slopes and valleys that had once been ours; at the corn and wheat growing upon the ground that had once been our hunting grounds; at the quietly flowing streams that we had used so often for watering places in the days so long gone by; my heart was very sad. Yet I've found that spot and am satisfied. I can now go back to the South and feel that my greatest desire has been granted."

When asked if the Indians of today followed many of the customs of their ancestors, he answered that they did not. Occasionally the older Indians, in memory of the days of their supremacy, dressed themselves to correspond and acted as in other days, but the younger generation knows nothing of those things and is as the white man. In Oklahoma they go to school, later engage in farming, or enter business. "Civilization has done much for them," said Gray Eagle. "They are hard workers and have ambitions to accomplish great things and be better citizens. Only we old Indians, who remember the strenuous times of the early days, have the wild blood in our veins. The younger ones have never even seen a buffalo."

Then he told of his early life in the county and related interesting stories of the past—Gray Eagle, the Indian chief, and John Williamson, the pioneer, talking together, at times, in a tongue that to us was strange, but to them an echo of a very real past.

The Loup he called Potato Water, because of the many wild potatoes that formerly grew upon its banks. Horse creek he remembered as Skeleton Water, the Pawnees one time having fought a band of Sioux on its banks. They were victorious but lost many warriors. Their own dead they buried, leaving the bodies of their enemies to decay in the sun. Soon the banks of the creek were strewn with skeletons and ever after the creek was known to the Indians as Skeleton Water. The Cedar was known as Willow creek, Council creek as the Skidi, and the Beaver as the Sandburr.

EARLY INDIAN HISTORY

BY MRS. SARAH CLAPP

In 1843 Mr. and Mrs. Lester W. Platt were first engaged in missionary work among the Pawnees, and in 1857 the government set aside a tract of land thirty miles by fifteen miles, in the rich prairie soil of Nance county, for their use; and when the Indian school was established at Genoa, Mrs. Platt was made matron or superintendent.

My mother taught in this school during the years 1866-67. She found the work interesting, learned much of the customs and legends of the Pawnees and grew very fond of that noble woman, Mrs. Platt, who was able to tell thrilling stories of her experiences during her mission work among the members of that tribe.

At the time my mother taught in the Genoa school, the Sioux, who were the greatest enemies of the Pawnees, on account of wanting to hunt in the same territory, were supposed to be friendly with the settlers, but drove away their horses and cattle and stole everything in sight, furnishing much excitement.

My father, Captain S. E. Cushing, accompanied my uncle, Major Frank North, on a number of expeditions against the hostile Indians, during the years 1869 until 1877. He was with Major North at the time of the famous charge on the village of the

114

Cheyennes, when the notorious chief, Tall Bull, was killed by my uncle.

In 1856, when Frank North came to Nebraska, a young boy, he mingled fearlessly with the Indians along the Missouri in the region of Omaha, where our family first settled, learning their mode of warfare and living, and their language, which he spoke as fluently as his mother tongue. In 1861 he took a position as clerk and interpreter at the Pawnee reservation and by 1863 he had become known as a daring scout.

The next year the building of the Union Pacific railroad was started, and as the work progressed westward the fierce Arapahoes, Cheyennes, and Sioux began attacking the laborers, until it seemed deadly peril to venture outside the camps. It was useless to call on the regular troops for help as the government needed them all to hold in check the armies of Lee and Johnston. A clipping from the Washington *Sunday Herald*, on this subject, states that "a happy thought occurred to Mr. Oakes Ames," the main spirit of the work. He sent a trusty agent to hunt up Frank North, who was then twenty-four years old. "What can be done to protect our working parties, Mr. North?" said Mr. Ames. "I have an idea," Mr. North answered. "If the authorities at Washington will allow me to organize a battalion of Pawnees and mount and equip them, I will undertake to picket your entire line and keep off other Indians.

"The Pawnees are the natural enemies of all the tribes that are giving you so much trouble, and a little encouragement and drill will make them the best irregular horse you could desire."

This plan was new but looked feasible. Accordingly Mr. Ames went to Washington, and, after some effort, succeeded in getting permission to organize a battalion of four hundred Pawnee warriors, who should be armed as were the U.S. cavalry and drilled in such simple tactics as the service required, and my uncle was commissioned a major of volunteers and ordered to command them. The newspaper clipping also says: "It would be difficult to estimate the service of Major North in money value." General Crook once said, in speaking of him, "Millions of government

115

property and hundreds of lives were saved by him on the line of the Union Pacific railroad, and on the Nebraska, Wyoming, and Montana frontiers."

There is much to be said in his praise, but I did not intend writing a eulogy, rather to tell of the stories which have come down to me, with which he and my other relatives were so closely connected.

During the many skirmishes and battles fought by the Pawnees, under Major North, he never lost a man; moreover, on several different occasions he passed through such hair-breadth escapes that the Pawnees thought him invulnerable. In one instance, while pursuing the retreating enemy, he discovered that his command had fallen back, and he was separated from them by over a mile. The enemy, discovering his plight, turned on him. He dismounted, being fully armed, and by using his horse as a breastwork he managed to reach his troops again, though his faithful horse was killed. This and many like experiences caused the Pawnees to believe that their revered leader led a charmed life. He never deceived them, and they loved to call him "Little Pawnee Le-Sharo" (Pawnee Chief), and so he was known as the White Chief of the Pawnees.

The coming of the railroad through the state, bringing thousands of settlers with household furnishings and machinery for tilling the soil, was of the greatest importance. It was concerning the guarding of that right of way that a writer for the *Horse World* has some interesting memories and devotes an article in a number in February, 1896, to the stories of Colonel W. F. Cody, Major Frank North, Captain Charles Morse, Captain Luther North, Captain Fred Mathews, and my father, Captain S. E. Cushing. The correspondent was under my father, in Company B, during one of the scouting expeditions, when the company was sent to guard O'Fallon's Bluffs, west of Fort McPherson on the Union Pacific. He tells much more of camp activities and of his initiation into border life than of the skirmishes or scouting trips. He was fond of horses and tells of a memorable race in which a horse of Buffalo Bill's was beaten by my father's horse "Jack."

My uncle, Captain Luther North, who also commanded a company of scouts at that time, now resides in Omaha.

While yet a boy he freighted between Omaha and Columbus and carried the mail, by pony, during a period when my grandmother felt that when she bade him good-bye in the morning she might never see him again, so unsettled was the feeling about the Indians. He was intimately acquainted with every phase of Indian life. He knew their pastimes and games, work of the medicine men and magicians, and especially was he familiar with many of their legends. I am happy to have been one of the children who often gathered 'round him to listen to the tales of his own experiences or stories told him by the red men.

One personal experience in the family happened before the building of the railroad, probably in sixty-one or sixty-two. A number of men, accompanied by the wives of two of them, went to put up hay for the government, on land located between Genoa and Monroe. One night the Indians surrounded their camp, presumably to drive away their stock. Naturally, the party rebelled, and during the melee which followed, Adam Smith and another man were killed and one of the women, Mrs. Murray, was wounded but saved herself by crawling away through the tall grass. The recital of this trouble grew in magnitude the farther it traveled, until people grew frantic with fear, believing it to mean an uprising of the Sioux. The settlers from Shell creek and all directions, bringing horses, cattle, and even their fowls, together with personal belongings, flocked into the village of Columbus for mutual protection. My mother, then a young girl, describes the first night as one of much confusion.

Some of the fugitives were sheltered with friends, others camped in the open. Animals, feeling as strange as did their masters, were bawling or screeching, and no one could sleep, as the greatest excitement prevailed.

117

"They built a stockade of upright posts about eight feet high, around the town," says my uncle Luther, thinking that as the Indians usually fought on horseback, this would be a great help if not a first-class fort.

They organized a militia company and men were detailed for guard duty and stationed at different points along the stockade, so serious seemed the situation. One night Luther North and two other young men were sent on picket duty outside the stockade. They took their horses and blankets and went up west of town about half a mile, to keep an eye on the surrounding country. A Mr. Needham had gone up to his farm (now the John Dawson farm) that day and did not return until it was getting dark. The guards thought it would be great fun to give him a little scare, so as he approached, they wrapped themselves in their blankets, mounted, and rode down under a bank. Just as he passed, they came up in sight and gave the Indian war whoop and started after him. He whipped his team into a run; they chased him, yelling at every step, but stopped a reasonable distance from the stockade and then went back. Mr. Needham gave graphic description of how the Indians had chased him, which so upset the entire population that sleep was out of the question that night. Moreover, he cautioned his wife in this wise: "Now, Christina, if the Indians come, it is everybody for himself, and you will have to skulk." This remark made by Mr. Needham became a byword, and even down into the next generation was a favorite saying and always provoked a smile. The young guards had no fear whatever of marauding Indians, and, blissfully unaware of the commotion they had aroused, went back up the road to a melon patch, ate a sufficient amount of the luscious fruit, picketed their horses, wrapped themselves in their blankets, and lay them down to pleasant dreams. The next morning, they rode into town and reported no red men in sight. After a few weeks, when there was no further evidence of trouble from the savages, the people gradually dispersed to their homes and farms which were, by that time, much in need of attention.

Major Frank Joshua North is best known for his organization of a group of Pawnee scouts and was instrumental in the Indian Wars, protecting the wagon trains and later the railroad crews during the construction of the transcontinental railroad.

Born in Ludlowville, NY, on March 10, 1840, his family moved to Ohio when Frank was just two years old. They moved again in 1856 to Nebraska, where the 16-year-old worked as a transporter, moving goods between Omaha and Fort Kearny.

It was in this capacity that North first made contact with the local Pawnee Indians. He soon learned their language so well, that by `860, he was working at the Pawnee Reservation near Fullerton, Nebraska as a clerk in their trading post. Later he became so proficient in the language that he worked as an interpreter.

In 1864 he accompanied the first Pawnee Scouts to the field under General Samuel R Curtis in an unsuccessful campaign against the Sioux. Curtis was so impressed with his knowledge of the Pawnee, that he suggested North organize a company of Pawnee Scouts to help the army during the Indian wars. When North agreed, he was given the ran of lieutenant. For the next 13 years North would lead the scouts in a number of campaigns against the Plains Indians, serving in Nebraska, Kansas, and Wyoming, receiving promotions to captain and then to major.

But by 1877 the Plains Indians had all but been subdued and North and his scouts were mustered out for the last time.

North then went into partnership with William F. "Buffalo Bill" Cody in a cattle ranch at the head of Dismal River in Western Nebraska. When the pair sold the business in 1882 then served one term in the Nebraska Legislature before joining up with Buffalo Bill's Wild West Show as its Indian Manager.

In 1884 he was severely injured in a riding accident in Hartford, Connecticut. He was brought home to Columbus, Nebraska, where he continued to suffer from the injuries until he died on March 14, 1885. [11]

---

[11] https://www.legendsofamerica.com/frank-north/

THE BLIZZARD OF 1888

BY MINNIE FREEMAN PENNEY

On January 12, 1888, the states of Nebraska and South Dakota were visited by a blizzard so fierce and cruel and death-dealing that residents of those sections cannot speak of it even now without an involuntary shudder.

The storm burst with great suddenness and fury, and many there were who did not live to tell the story of their suffering. And none suffered more keenly than did the occupants of the prairie schoolhouses. Teachers and pupils lost their lives or were terribly maimed. The great storm indicated most impressively the measure of danger and trial that must be endured by the country school teacher in the isolated places on the frontier.

Three Nebraska country school teachers—Loie Royce of Plainfield, Etta Shattuck of Holt county, and Minnie Freeman of Mira Valley, were the subjects of much newspaper writing.

Miss Royce had nine pupils. Six went home for luncheon and remained on account of the storm. The three remaining pupils with the teacher stayed in the schoolhouse until three o'clock. Their fuel gave out, and as her boarding house was but fifteen rods away, the teacher decided to take the children home with her.

In the fury of the storm they wandered and were lost. Darkness came, and with it death. One little boy sank into the eternal silence. The brave little teacher stretched herself out on the cold ground and cuddled the two remaining ones closer. Then the other little boy died and at daylight the spirit of the little girl, aged seven, fluttered away, leaving the young teacher frozen and dumb with agony. Loie Royce "hath done what she could; angels can do no better." Miss Royce lost both feet by amputation.

Etta Shattuck, after sending her children home (all living near) tried to go to her home. Losing her way, she took refuge in a haystack, where she remained, helpless and hungry Friday, Saturday, and Sunday, suffering intensely and not able to move. She lived but a short time after her terrible experience.

Minnie Freeman was teaching in Mira Valley, Valley county. She had in her charge seventeen pupils. Finding it impossible to remain in the schoolhouse, she took the children with her to her boarding place almost a mile from the schoolhouse.

Words are useless in the effort to portray that journey to the safe shelter of the farmhouse, with the touching obedience of the children to every word of direction—rather *felt* than *heard*, in that fierce winding-sheet of ice and snow. How it cut and almost blinded them! It was terrible on their eyes. They beat their way onward, groping blindly in the darkness, with the visions of life and death ever before the young teacher responsible for the destiny of seventeen souls.

All reached the farmhouse and were given a nice warm supper prepared by the hostess and the teacher, and comfortable beds provided.

Minnie Freeman was unconscious of anything heroic or unusual. Doing it in the simple line of duty to those placed in her care, she still maintains that it was the trust placed in the Great Spirit who guides and cares for His own which led the little band—

"Through the desert and illimitable air,
Lone wandering, but not lost."

Many details of Freeman's early life have been lost to history, but she was born in 1867 or 1868 in Pennsylvania or New York, one of four children to William and Sarah Freeman. The family moved to Nebraska in 1871, settling in Howard County at a time when the adjacent Nance County was a Pawnee Indian reservation.

Gayle Biddle Swicker, another great-granddaughter, shared anecdotes about Freeman's childhood that have been passed down three or more generations.

"They were among the first settlers in Nebraska," said Ms. Swicker, 62, "and if I've got the story right, she'd hide under her mother's skirt when the Indians came by asking for food because they were in a forced migration to a new reservation and they were starving."

Beyond Freeman's career as a schoolteacher, she was a political and social activist in Nebraska and Chicago at a time when female public figures were few and far between.

According to several newspapers, she was the first Republican national committeewoman to represent Nebraska; the first president of the Nebraska American Legion Auxiliary; state president of the Federation of Women's clubs; part of the team that established a new Nebraska

123

state seal; and a delegate, appointed by two of Nebraska's governors, to local and national conferences. Freeman died on Nov. 1, 1943, in Chicago. She was believed to be 75.

Her resourceful and dramatic rescue is immortalized in a Victorian parlor song by the composer William Vincent, "Thirteen Were Saved; Or Nebraska's Fearless Maid." The original sheet music is at History Nebraska, the state's historical society.[12]

---

[12] https://www.nytimes.com/2018/10/03/obituaries/minnie-mae-freeman-penney-overlooked.html

MY TRIP WEST IN 1861

BY SARAH SCHOOLEY RANDALL

In 1857 my brother, Charles A. Schooley, landed at Brownville and soon after purchased several tracts of land near there, one being the old home of Church Howe and adjoining the present site of the village of Howe. Incidentally, my husband's father, N. G. Randall, three years later purchased land within three miles—known later as Bedford.

In 1860, while my brother was visiting his old home, White Deer Valley, near Williamsport, Pennsylvania, the smoldering flames of adventure were kindled in my mind which nothing but a trip west could quench. On March 1, 1861, we left Williamsport by train from Pittsburgh and on arriving there went to the Monongahela hotel, then a magnificent building. Abe Lincoln had just left the hotel, much to our disappointment. After a few days we engaged passage on the *Argonaut* to St. Louis via the Monongahela, the Ohio, and the Mississippi rivers. Our experiences were varied and exciting enough to meet my expectations. During one night we stood tied to a tree and another night the pumps were kept going to keep us from sinking. Small consolation we got from the captain's remark that this was "the last trip for this old hulk." We had ample time for seeing all the important cities along the shore—Cincinnati, Louisville, etc.

Arriving at St. Louis we took passage on a new boat, *Sunshine*, and set sail upstream. Perhaps we felt a few pangs of fear as we neared the real pioneer life. We changed boats again at St. Joe and then our trip continued, now up the treacherous Missouri. Every now and then we struck a snag which sent the dishes scurrying from the table. I am reminded that this trip was typical of our lives: floating downstream is easy but upstream is where we strike the snags.

Of our valued acquaintances met on the trip were Rev. and Mrs. Barrette, the former a Presbyterian minister coming to Brownville, and our friendship continued after reaching our destination. Arriving in Brownville, we went to the McPherson hotel, where we continued to hear disturbing rumors about the coming civil war.

After a few days we took a carriage and went west ten miles over the beautiful rolling prairies to our ranch. I was charmed with the scene, which was vastly different from the mountains and narrow winding valleys of Pennsylvania, and was determined to stay, though my brother had lost his enthusiasm and gave me two weeks to change my mind. Many a homesick spell I had when I would have very quickly returned to my father's home of peace and plenty, but the danger of travel detained me. I assured my brother that if he would only stay I would be very brave and economical. I only wanted five small rooms plainly furnished and a horse and carriage. When the place was ready, we left Brownville in a big wagon, drawn by oxen, and fortified by a load of provisions. When we came in sight of our bungalow it proved to be a one-room, unpainted and unplastered edifice, but I soon overcame that defect by the use of curtains, and as all lived alike then, we were content with our surroundings. Our first callers were three hundred Indians on an expedition. I had been reading extensively about Indians, so knew when I saw their squaws and papooses with them that they were friendly—in fact, rather too familiar.

My brother fenced his land and planted it in corn and all kinds of vegetables. The season being favorable there was an abundant crop, both cultivated and wild. The timber abounded with grapes,

126

plums, nuts, etc., and strawberries on the prairies. We had a well of fine water, a good cellar or cave, and a genuine "creampot" cow. Instead of a carriage I had a fine saddle horse (afterwards sold to a captain in the army), and how we did gallop over the prairies! One of my escapades was to a neighbor's home ten miles away for ripe tomatoes. In lieu of a sack we tied together the neck and sleeves of a calico wrapper, filled it with the tomatoes, then tied the bottom and balanced it astride the horse in front of me. Going through the tall slough grass in one place near Sheridan, now Auburn, the horse became frantic with heat and flies and attempted to run away. The strings gave way and the tomatoes scattered. Finally, the saddle turned, and the well-trained horse stopped. An inventory revealed one sleeve full of tomatoes remaining.

Among our near neighbors were Mr. and Mrs. Milo Gates and family, and Mr. and Mrs. Engle. Mrs. Gates's cheerful optimism made this pioneer life not only possible but enjoyable.

After five months, my brother joined the army and went south as a captain; was several times promoted and stayed all through the war. A year after I went back to Brownville to stay until the war was over, and there made many valued acquaintances: Senator Tipton's sister, Mrs. Atkinson, Judge Wheeler, H. C. Lett, the McCrearys, Hackers, Whitneys, Carsons, Dr. Guin, Furnas, Johnson, etc. About this time the citizens gave a party for the boys who enlisted, and there I met E. J. Randall, whom I married soon after he returned from the army. Of the four Randall brothers who enlisted one was killed, one wounded, and one taken prisoner. Two of them still live, Dr. H. L. Randall of Aurora, forty-seven years a practicing physician in Nebraska and at one time surgeon at the Soldiers' Home, Grand Island; and A. D. Randall of Chapman, Nebraska, who enlisted at the age of sixteen and served all through the war.

After a college course of four years my husband entered the ministry and served for twenty-five years in Nebraska, except for one year of mission work at Cheyenne, Wyoming. The itinerant life is not unlike the pioneer life and brought with it the bitter and

127

sweet as well, but the bitter was soon forgotten and blessed memories remain of the dear friends scattered all over the state of Nebraska, and indeed to the ends of the earth.

Dr. Wharton said when paying his tribute to my departed husband, "He still lives on in the lives of those to whom he has ministered." Our children are Charles H. Randall of Los Angeles, California, member of congress, and Mrs. Anna Randall Pope of Lincoln, Nebraska.

STIRRING EVENTS ALONG THE LITTLE BLUE

BY CLARENDON E. ADAMS

Painting a Buffalo

The following narrative of Albert Bierstadt's visit to what is now Nuckolls county, Nebraska, was told to me by Mr. E. S. Comstock, a pioneer of the county. Mr. Comstock made his first settlement in this county at Oak Grove, in 1858, and was in charge of the Oak Grove ranch when this incident took place.

In 1863 Mr. Bierstadt returned from the Pacific coast via the Overland stage route, which was then conducted by Russell, Majors & Waddell, the pioneer stage and pony expressmen of the plains. Arriving at Oak Grove ranch, Mr. Bierstadt and his traveling companion, a Mr. Dunlap, correspondent of the New York *Post*, decided to stop a few days and have a buffalo hunt. In company with E. S. Comstock, his son George, and a neighbor by the name of Eubanks, who was killed by the Indians the next year, they proceeded to the Republican Valley and camped the first night in the grove on Lost creek, now known as Lincoln Park. The following morning the party proceeded up the river to the farm now owned by Frank Schmeling. Here they discovered a large herd of buffalo grazing along the creek to the west and covering

129

the prairies to the north for several miles. Mr. Comstock says that it was one of the largest herds of buffalo he had ever encountered, and that Mr. Bierstadt became greatly excited and said, "Now, boys, is our time for fun. I want to see an enraged wounded buffalo. I want to see him so mad that he will bellow and tear up the ground." Mr. Comstock said they arranged for the affray: Mr. Bierstadt was to take his position on a small knoll to the east of the herd, fix himself with his easel so that he could sketch the landscape and the grazing bison, and when this was done the wounding of one of the buffalo bulls was to take place.

Bierstadt was stationed on a small knoll in plain view of the herd; Mr. Eubanks was stationed in a draw near Bierstadt, in order to protect him from the charges of the buffalo, if necessary. George Comstock was to select a buffalo bull from the herd and wound him and then tantalize him by shaking a red blanket at him until he was thoroughly enraged, then he was to give him another wound from his rifle and lead out in the direction of Mr. Bierstadt.

The wounded buffalo became furious and charged Comstock's horse repeatedly, but Comstock, being an expert horseman, evaded the fierce charges and was all the time coming nearer to Bierstadt. When within about three hundred yards Comstock whirled his horse to the side of the maddened monster. As a buffalo does not see well out of the side of his eyes on account of the long shaggy hair about the face, Comstock was lost to his view. The infuriated animal tossed his head high in air and the only thing he saw was Bierstadt. Onward he rushed toward the artist, pawing the ground and bellowing furiously. Bierstadt called for help and took to his heels. The buffalo struck the easel and sent it in splinters through the air. Onward he rushed after the fleeing artist, who was making the best time of his life. Mr. Comstock said he was running so fast that his coat tails stuck so straight out that you could have played a game of euchre on them. The buffalo was gaining at every jump.

At this point in his story Mr. Comstock became greatly excited. He was standing on the identical spot telling me the story and was living the exciting scene over again. "Why," he said, "I thought

130

Eubanks never would shoot. I was scared. The buffalo nearly had his horns under Bierstadt's coat tail. He was snorting froth and blood all over him, but the gun cracked, and the buffalo fell and Bierstadt was so overcome he fell at the same time entirely exhausted but saved from a fearful death." When he recovered sufficiently to talk, he said, "That's enough; no more wounded buffalo for me." Mr. Bierstadt was several days recovering from his fearful experience, but while he was recovering, he was painting the picture. "Mr. Dunlap, the correspondent, wrote a graphic and vivid pen picture of the exciting scene," said Mr. Comstock; "but when Mr. Bierstadt finished his picture of the infuriated charging buffalo and the chase, the pen picture was not in it."

This was the painting that brought Bierstadt into prominence as an artist. It was exhibited at the first Chicago exhibition and was sold for $75,000. I saw the picture in Chicago before I heard Mr. Comstock's narrative, and as I was one of the owners of El Capitan Rancho, the landscape of the famous painting, I fixed his story vividly upon my memory. Mr. Mike Woerner now owns a portion of El Capitan Rancho, the landscape of this famous painting. A portion of this original painting is embraced in Mr. Bierstadt's masterpiece, "The Last of the Buffalo."

[Bierstad's] rugged, romanticized landscapes of the West, painted on a grand scale with an abundance of detail and dramatic lighting, captured the imagination of 19th-century art collectors and their interest catapulted Bierstadt to the top of the American art market. His paintings brought record prices in his lifetime. Bierstadt enjoyed tremendous success and recognition.[13]

An Indian Raid

The settlement of the section now included in Nuckolls county was attended with more privation and suffering from Indian raids

---

[13] https://www.albertbierstadt.org/biography.html

and depredations than any other county in the state of Nebraska. The great Indian raids of August 7, 1864 extended from Denver, Colorado, to Gage county, Nebraska, at which time every stage station and settlement along the entire line of the Overland trail was included in that skillfully planned attack. A certain number of warriors were assigned to each place and the attack was simultaneous along the line for four hundred miles in extent.

The Oak Grove ranch was among the most formidable in fortifications and a band of forty well-armed braves was sent to capture and destroy it. On the day of the attack G. S. Comstock, owner of Oak Grove ranch, was away from home; but besides his family there were five men at the stockade. The Indians came to the ranch about mid-day in a friendly attitude. They had left their ponies about a quarter of a mile away. They asked for something to eat and were permitted to come into the house with their guns and bows and arrows on their persons. They finished their dinner, and each received a portion of tobacco and some matches. Then without any warning they turned upon the inmates of the ranch yelling and shooting like demons, and only for the quickness and great presence of mind of one of the Comstock boys the whites would all have been killed or taken away captives to submit to the cruelty of the savage foe.

A Mr. Kelly, from Beatrice, was there and was the first to fall pierced with an arrow. He had a navy revolver in his belt. The Indians rushed for it, but young Comstock was too quick for them and seized the revolver first and shot down the leader of the braves. Seeing the fate of their leader, the Indians rushed to the door in great fright. The revolver was in skillful hands and three more of the braves went down under the unerring aim of young Comstock. Kelly and Butler were both killed outright. Two men by the name of Ostrander and a boy were wounded. All the other occupants of the ranch had their clothes pierced with arrows or bullets.

The Indians ran to their ponies, and while they were away planning another attack, the wounded were cared for as best they could. The doors were securely barred, and the living were stationed in the most advantageous places for defense. The friendly game of the Indians had not worked as they expected, but they were not daunted and soon they encircled the house, riding, shooting, and yelling. This fiendish warfare they kept up all the afternoon. They tried several times to set the buildings on fire but shots from experienced marksmen, both men and women, kept them at bay.

The new leader of the Indians rode a white pony and seemed at times to work his warriors up to great desperation, and young Comstock made up his mind to shoot him the next time that he appeared. It was now too dark to distinguish one man from another. Mr. Comstock, senior, was mounted on a white horse and he was enroute home about the time the Indians were expected to return. The vigilant son raised his gun, took aim, and was about to shoot, when one of the girls, remembering that her father rode a white horse, called out, "Father, is it you?" An affirmative answer came back just in time to prevent the fatal shot which would have followed in an instant more. Mr. Comstock had ridden through the Indian lines, while returning to his ranch, unmolested. He said to me he believed the Indians spared his life that evening on account of favors he had always granted them.

Five miles east of the Comstock ranch that day a boy eighteen years old by the name of Ulig was met by two Indians. One of them shook hands with him while the other pierced his body with a spear and then scalped him and left him writhing in the broiling sun to die on the prairie. This savage and brutal act was followed by others unparalleled even in savage warfare. Four miles above Oak Grove at a place called the Narrows on the Little Blue river, lived a family of ten persons by the name of Eubanks. They were from the East and knew nothing of Indians' cruel warfare and when they were attacked, they left their cabin and ran for the trees and brush along the river banks. Nine of them were murdered in the most brutal manner: scalped and stripped of their clothing. Two of the women, Mrs. Eubanks, with a young babe in her arms, and Laura Roper, a school teacher who was there on a visit, were the only ones who arrived at a place of concealment and would have escaped had not the babe from heat and fright cried out. The practiced ear of the Indians caught the sound, and they were made captives and subjected to the most inhuman and beastly treatment by the horrible savages. After the mother was made a captive the baby cried from hunger. The mother was so famished she could not nourish the babe but held it fondly in her arms trying to soothe it; and one of the merciless savages stepped up and brained it with his tomahawk. No pen or brush can tell the horrors of this diabolical deed.

The two women were subjected to six months of bondage impossible to describe. I was telling this story one day to the late Captain Henry E. Palmer of Omaha, and learned from him that he and his command of soldiers and Pawnee scouts followed these inhuman wretches over the plains trying to bring them to bay, and finally down on the Solomon river in Kansas captured some of the Indian chiefs and succeeded in exchanging them for the two women captives.

This is one of the terrible chapters in the early settlement of Nuckolls county and was graphically detailed to me by Mr. Comstock soon after I settled in the county.

There is a Monument erected on the Oregon Trail by Nuckolls County Nebraska in memory of those who were killed and those who escaped at the Oak Grove Ranch in the Indian Raid, August 7, 1864.[14]

---

[14] https://www.nps.gov/places/000/oak-grove-station-comstock-ranch.htm

MY LAST BUFFALO HUNT

BY J. STERLING MORTON

(Read before the Nebraska State Historical Society, January 10, 1899)

Among all the glowing and glorious autumns of the forty-odd which I have enjoyed in clear-skied Nebraska, the most delicious, dreamy, and tranquil was that of 1861. The first day of October in that year surpassed in purity of air, clouds, and coloring all the other October days in my whole life. The prairies were not a somber brown, but a gorgeous old-gold; and there drifted in the dry, crisp atmosphere lace-like fragments of opalescent clouds which later in the afternoon gave the horizon the look of a far-away ocean upon which one could see fairy ships, and upon its farther-away shores splendid castles, their minarets and towers tipped with gold. The indolence of savagery saturated every inhalation, and all physical exertion except in the hunt or chase seemed repellant, irksome, and unendurable.

Then it was that—like an evolution from environment—the desire and impulse to go upon a buffalo hunt seized upon and held and encompassed and dominated every fibre of my physical, every ambition and aspiration of my mental, make-up. Controlled by this spontaneous reincarnation of the barbaric tastes and habits of some nomadic ancestor of a prehistoric generation, arrangements for an

136

excursion to Fort Kearny on the Platte (Colonel Alexander, of the regular army, then in command) were completed. With food rations, tent and camping furniture, and arms and ammunition, and pipes and tobacco, and a few drops of distilled rye (to be used only when snake-bitten), a light one-horse wagon drawn by a well-bred horse which was driven by the writer, was early the next morning leaving Arbor Lodge, and briskly speeding westward on the "Overland Trail" leading to California. And what rare roads there were in those buoyant days of the pioneers! All the prairies, clear across the plains from the Missouri river to the mountains, were perfectly paved with solid, tough, but elastic sod. And no asphalt or block-paved avenue or well-worked pike can give the responsive pressure to the touch of a human foot or a horse-hoof that came always from those smooth and comely trails. Especially in riding on horseback were the felicities of those primitive prairie roads emphasized and accentuated. Upon them one felt the magnetism and life of his horse; they animated and electrified him with the vigor and spirit of the animal until in elation, the rider became, at least emotionally, a centaur—a semi-horse human. The invigoration and exaltation of careering over undulating prairies on a beautiful, speedy, and spirited horse thrilled every sense and satisfied, as to exhilaration, by physical exercise, the entire mental personality. Nature's roads in Nebraska are unequaled by any of their successors.

This excursion was in a wagon without springs; and after driving alone, as far as the Weeping Water crossing, I overtook an ox train loaded with goods and supplies for Gilman's ranch on the Platte away beyond Fort Kearny.

One of the proprietors, Mr. Jed Gilman, was in command of the outfit, and by his cordial and hospitable invitation I became his willing and voracious guest for the noonday meal. With a township for a dining room over which arched the turquoise-colored sky, like a vaulted ceiling, frescoed with clouds of fleecy white, we sat down upon our buffalo robes to partake of a hearty meal. There was no white settler within miles of our camp. The cry of "Dinner is now ready in the next car" had never been heard west of the

137

Mississippi river nor even dreamed of in the East. The bill of fare was substantial: bacon fried, hot bread, strong coffee, stronger raw onions, and roasted potatoes. And the appetite which made all exquisitely palatable and delicious descended to us out of the pure air and the exhilaration of perfect health. And then came the post-prandial pipe—how fragrant and solacing its fumes—from Virginia natural leaf, compared to which the exhalations from a perfecto cigar are today a disagreeable stench. There was then the leisure to smoke, the liberty and impulse to sing, to whoop, and to generally simulate the savages into whose hunting grounds we were making an excursion. Life lengthened out before us like the Overland route to the Pacific in undulations of continuously rising hillocks and from the summit of each one scaled we saw a similarly attractive one beyond in a seemingly never-ending pathway of pleasure, ambition, and satisfaction. The gold of the Pacific coast was not more real then than the invisible possibilities of life, prosperity, success, and contentment which were to teem, thrive, and abound upon these prairies which seemed only farms asleep or like thoughts unuttered—books unopened.

But the smoke over, the oxen again yoked to the wagons and the train, like a file of huge white beetles, lumbered along to the songs, swearing, and whip-crackings of the drivers toward the crossing of Salt creek. However, by my persuasive insistence, Mr. Gilman left his wagon boss in charge and getting into my wagon accompanied me. Together we traveled briskly until quite late at night when we made camp at a point near where the town of Wahoo now stands. There was a rough ranch cabin there, and we remained until the following morning, when we struck out at a brisk trot toward Fort Kearny, entering the Platte Valley at McCabe's ranch. The day and the road were perfect. We made good time. At night we were entertained at Warfield's, on the Platte. The water in the well there was too highly flavored to be refreshing. Nine skunks had been lifted out of it the day of our arrival and only Platte river water could be had, which we found rather stale for having been hauled some distance in an old sorghum cask. But fatigue and a square meal are an innocent opiate, and we were soon fast asleep under the open sky with the moon and stars only to hear how loudly a big ranchman can snore in a bedroom of a million or more acres. In the morning of our third day out, we were up, breakfasted with the sunrise, and drove on over the then untried railroad bed of the Platte Valley at a rattling gait. The stanch and speedy animal over which the reins were drawn, a splendid bay of gentle birth, had courage and endurance by heredity, and thus we made time. Ranches were from twenty to thirty miles apart. And the night of the third day found us at Mabin's.

This was a hotel, feed barn, dry goods establishment, and saloon all under one roof, about thirty miles from Fort Kearny. After a reasonably edible supper, Mr. Gilman and I were escorted to the saloon and informed that we could repose and possibly sleep in the aisle which divided it from the granary which was filled with oats. Our blankets and buffalo robes were soon spread out in this narrow pathway. On our right were about two hundred bushels of oats in bulk, and on our left the counter which stood before variously shaped bottles containing alleged gin, supposed whiskey, and probable brandy. We had not been long in a recumbent position before—instead of sleep gently creeping over us—we experienced that we were race courses and grazing grounds for innumerable myriads of sand fleas. Immediately Gilman insisted that we should change our apartment and go out on the prairies near a haystack; but I stubbornly insisted that, as the fleas had not bitten me, I would continue indoors. Thereupon Gilman incontinently left, and then the fleas with vicious vigor and voracity assaulted me.

The bites were sharp, they were incisive and decisive. They came in volleys. Then in wrath I too arose from that lowly but lively couch between the oats and the bar and sullenly went out under the starlit sky to find Mr. Gilman energetically whipping his shirt over a wagon wheel to disinfest it from fleas. But the sand fleas of the Platte are not easily discharged or diverted from a fair and juicy victim. They have a wonderful tenacity of purpose. They trotted and hopped and skipped along behind us to the haystack. They affectionately and fervidly abided with us on the prairie; and it is safe to say that there never were two human beings more thoroughly perforated, more persistently punctured with flea bites than were the two guests at Mabins's ranch during all that long and agonizing night. However, there came an end to the darkness and the attempt at sleep, and after an early breakfast we resumed the Fort Kearny journey to arrive at its end in the late afternoon of the fourth day.

There I found Colonel Alexander, of the regular army, in command. John Heth, of Virginia, was the sutler for the post and after some consultation and advisement it was determined that we might without much danger from Indians go south to the Republican river for a buffalo hunt. At that time the Cheyennes, who were a bloodthirsty tribe, were in arms against the white people and yearning for their scalps wherever found. But to avoid or mitigate dangers Colonel Alexander considerately detailed Lieutenant Bush with twelve enlisted men, all soldiers of experience in the Indian country, to go with us to the Republican Valley as an escort or guard—in military parlance, on detached service. Thus, our party moved southward with ample force of arms for its defense.

The four hunters of the expedition were Lieutenant Bush, John Heth, John Talbot (who had been honorably discharged from the regular army after some years of service) and myself. The excursion was massed and ready for departure at 8 o'clock on the bright morning of October 6, 1861. The course taken was nearly due south from the present site of Kearney city in Buffalo county. The expedition consisted of two large army wagons, four mules attached to each wagon, a light, two-horse spring wagon, and four trained riding horses experienced in the chase, together with twelve soldiers of the regular U. S. army and the gentlemen already named. It had not traveled more than twenty-five miles south of Fort Kearny before it came in view of an immense and seemingly uncountable herd of buffalo.

My first sight of these primitive beeves of the plains I shall never forget. They were so distant that I could not make out their individual forms and I at once jumped to the conclusion that they were only an innumerable lot of crows sitting about upon the knobs and hillocks of the prairies. But in a few moments, when we came nearer, they materialized and were, sure enough, real bellowing, snorting, wallowing buffaloes. At first, they appeared to give no heed to our outfit, but after we saddled and mounted our horses and rode into their midst they began to scatter and to form into small bands, single file. The herd separated into long, black swaying strings and each string was headed by the best meat among its numbers. The leading animal was generally a three-year-old cow. Each of these strings, or single-file bands, ran in a general southeast direction and each of the four hunters—Bush, Heth, Talbot, and the writer—selected a string and went for the preeminent animal with enthusiasm, zeal, and impulsive foolhardiness.

In the beginning of the pell-mell, hurry-scurry race it seemed that it would be very easy to speedily overtake the desired individual buffalo that we intended to shoot and kill. The whole band seemed to run leisurely. They made a sort of sidewise gait, a movement such as one often sees in a dog running ahead of a wagon on a country road. Upon the level prairie we made very perceptible gains upon them, but when a declivity was reached and we made a down hill gallop we were obliged to rein in and hold up the horses, or take the chances of a broken leg or neck by being ditched in a badger or wolf hole. But the buffaloes, with their heavy shoulders and huge hair-matted heads, lumbered along down the incline with great celerity, gaining so much upon us that every now and then one of them would drop out from the line upon reaching an attractive depression, roll over two or three times in his "wallow," jump up and join his fleeing fellows before we could reach him.

But finally, after swinging and swaying hither and thither with the band or line as it swayed and swung, the lead animal was reached and with much exultation and six very nervous shots put to death. My trophy proved to be a buffalo cow of two or three years of age; and after she had dropped to the ground, a nimble

141

calf, about three months old, evidently her progeny, began making circles around and around the dead mother and bleating pitifully, enlarging the circle each time, until at last it went out of sight onto the prairie and alone, all the other parts of the herd having scattered beyond the rising bluffs and far away.

That afternoon was fuller of tense excitement, savage enthusiasms, zeal, and barbaric ambition than any other that could be assorted from my life of more than sixty years. There was a certain amount of ancestral heathenism aroused in every man, spurring a horse to greater swiftness, in that chase for large game. And there was imperial exultation of the primitive barbaric instinct when the game fell dead and its whooping captors surrounded its breathless carcass.

But the wastefulness of the buffalo hunter of those days was wicked beyond description and, because of its utter recklessness of the future, wholly unpardonable. Only the hump, ribs, the tongue, and perhaps now and then one hind-quarter were saved for use from each animal. The average number of pounds of meat saved from each buffalo killed between the years 1860 and 1870 would not exceed twenty. In truth, thousands of buffaloes were killed merely to get their tongues and pelts. The inexcusable and unnecessary extermination of those beef-producing and very valuable fur-bearing animals only illustrates the extravagance of thoughtlessness and mental nearsightedness in the American people when dealing with practical and far-reaching questions. It also demonstrates, in some degree, the incapacity of the ordinary every-day law-makers of the United States. Game laws have seldom been enacted in any of the states before the virtual extinction of the game they purposed to protect. Here in Nebraska among big game were many hundreds of thousands of buffaloes, tens of thousands of elk and deer and antelope, while among smaller game the wild turkey and the prairie chicken were innumerable. But today Nebraska game is practically extinct. Even the prairie chicken and the wild turkey are seldom found anywhere along the Missouri bluffs in the southern and eastern part of the commonwealth.

142

Looking back: what might have been accomplished for the conservation of game in the trans-Missouri country is suggested so forcibly that one wonders at the stupendous stupidity which indolently permitted its destruction.

The first night outward and southeastward from Fort Kearny we came to Turkey creek which empties into the Republican river. There, after dark, tents were pitched at a point near the place where the government in previous years established kilns and burned lime for the use of soldiers in building quarters for themselves and the officers at Fort Kearny which was constructed in 1847 by Stewart L. Van Vliet, now a retired brigadier general and the oldest living graduate of West Point. After a sumptuous feast of buffalo steak, a strong pint of black coffee and a few pipes of good tobacco, our party retired; sleep came with celerity and the camp was peacefully at rest, with the exception of two regular soldiers who stood guard until 12 o'clock, and were then relieved by two others who kept vigil until sunrise. At intervals I awoke during the night and listened to the industrious beavers building dams on the creek. They were shoveling mud with their trowel-shaped tails into the crevices of their dams with a constantly-resounding slapping and splashing all night. The architecture of the beaver is not unlike that which follows him and exalts itself in the chinked and daubed cabins of the pioneers.

The darkness was followed by a dawn of beauty and breakfast came soon thereafter, and for the first time my eyes looked out upon the attractive, fertile, and beautiful valley of the Republican river. All that delightful and invigorating day we zealously hunted. We found, occasionally, small bands of buffaloes here and there among the bluffs and hills along the valley of the Republican. But these animals were generally aged and of inferior quality. Besides such hunting, we found a great quantity of blue-winged and green-winged teal in the waters of the Republican and bagged not a few of them. There is no water-fowl, in my judgment, not even the redheaded duck and canvasback duck, which excels in delicate tissue and flavor the delicious teal.

143

Just a little before sundown, on the third day of our encampment, by the bluffs land of the Republican, Lieutenant Bush and Mr. Heth in one party, and John Talbot and I in another, were exploring the steep, wooded bluffs which skirted the valley. The timber growing at that time on the sides of these bluffs was, much of it, of very good size and I shall never forget going down a precipitous path along the face of a hill and suddenly coming upon a strange and ghastly sight among the top limbs and branches of an oak tree which sprang from the rich soil of a lower level. The weird object which then impressed itself upon my memory forever was a dead Indian sitting upright in a sort of wicker-work coffin which was secured by thongs to the main trunk of the tree. The robe with which he had been clothed had been torn away by buzzards and only the denuded skeleton sat there. The bleached skull leered and grinned at me as though the savage instinct to repulse an intruder from their hunting grounds still lingered in the fleshless head. Perfectly I recall the long scalp-lock, floating in the wind, and the sense of dread and repellant fear which, for the startled moment, took possession of me in the presence of this arboreally interred Indian whose remains had been stored away in a tree-top instead of having been buried in the ground.

Not long after this incident we four came together again down in the valley at a great plum orchard. The plum trees covered an area of several acres; they stood exceedingly close together. The frosts had been just severe enough to drop the fruit onto the ground. Never before nor since have my eyes beheld or my palate tasted as luscious fruit as those large yellow and red plums which were found that afternoon lying in bushels in the valley of the Republican. While we were all seated upon the ground eating plums and praising their succulence and flavor, we heard the click-cluck of a turkey. Immediately we laid ourselves flat upon the earth and in the course of ten minutes beheld a procession of at least seventy-five wild turkeys feeding upon plums. We remained moveless and noiseless until those turkeys had flown up into the tall cottonwood trees standing thereabouts and gone to roost. Then after darkness had settled down upon the face of the earth we faintly discerned the black forms or hummocks of fat turkeys all

144

through the large and leafless limbs of the cottonwoods which had been nearly defoliated by the early frosts of October. It required no deft marksmanship or superior skill to bring down forty of those birds in a single evening. That number we took into camp. In quick time we had turkey roasted, turkey grilled, turkey broiled; and never have I since eaten any turkey so well flavored, so juicy and rich, as that fattened upon the wild plums of the Republican Valley in the year 1861.

At last, surfeited with hunting and its successes, we set out on our return to Fort Kearny. When about half way across the divide, a sergeant, one of the most experienced soldiers and plainsmen of the party, declared that he saw a small curl of smoke in the hazy distance and a little to the west and south of us. To my untrained eye the smoke was at first invisible, but with a field glass I ultimately discerned a delicate little blue thread hanging in the sky, which the soldiers pronounced smoke ascending from an Indian camp. Readjusting the glasses, I soon made out to see three Indians stretched by the fire seemingly asleep, while two were sitting by the embers apparently cooking, eating, and drinking. Very soon, however, the two feasters espied our wagons and party. Immediately they came running on foot to meet us; the other three, awaking, followed them; speedily they were in our midst. They proved, however, to be peaceful Pawnees. Mr. John Heth spoke the language of that tribe and I shall never forget the coolness with which these representatives of that nomadic race informed him that Mrs. Heth and his little two-years-of-age daughter, Minnie, were in good health in their wigwam at Fort Kearny; they were sure of it because they had looked into the window of the Heth home the day before and saw them eating and drinking their noonday meal.

These Indians then expressed a wish for some turkey feathers. They were told to help themselves. Immediately they pulled out a vast number of the large feathers of the wings and tails and decorated their own heads with them. The leader of the aboriginal expedition, in conversation with Mr. Heth, informed him that although they were on foot they carried the lariats which we saw hanging from their arms for the purpose of hitching onto and annexing some Cheyenne ponies which they were going south to steal. They walked away from home but intended to ride back. The barbaric commander in charge of this larcenous expedition was named "The Fox," and when questioned by Mr. Heth as to the danger of the enterprise, and informed that he might probably lose his life and get no ponies at all, Captain Fox smiled and said grimly that he knew he should ride back to the Pawnee village on the Loup the owner of good horses; that only a year or two before that time he had been alone down into the Cheyenne village and got a great many horses safely out and up onto the Loup fork among the Pawnees without losing a single one. "The Fox" admitted, however, that even in an expedition so successful as the one which he recalled there were a great many courage-testing inconveniences and annoyances. But he dwelt particularly upon the fact that the Cheyennes always kept their ponies in a corral which was in the very center of their village. The huts, habitations, tipis, and wigwams of the owners of the ponies were all constructed around their communal corral in a sort of a circle, but "The Fox" said that he nevertheless, in his individual excursion of which he proudly boasted, crawled during the middle of the night in among the ponies and was about to slip a lariat on the bell-mare without her stirring, when she gave a little jump, and the bell on her neck rang out pretty loudly. Then he laid down in the center of the herd and kept still, very still, while the horses walked over him and tramped upon him until he found it very unpleasant. But very soon he saw and heard some of the Cheyennes come out and look and walk about to see if anything was wrong. Then he said he had to stay still and silent under the horses' hoofs and make no noise or die and surely be scalped. At last, however, the Cheyennes, one after another, all went back into their wigwams to sleep, and then he very slowly and without a sound took the bell off from the mare, put his lariat on her neck quietly, led her out and all the herd of Cheyenne ponies followed. He never stopped until he was safe up north of the Platte river and had all his equine spoils safe in the valley of the Loup fork going towards the Pawnee village where Genoa now stands.

146

The Fox was an "expansionist" and an annexationist out of sympathy for the oppressed ponies of the Cheyennes.

The Fox declared that the number of horses he made requisition for at that time on the stables of the Cheyennes was three hundred. At this statement, some incredulity was shown by Mr. Heth, myself, and some others present. Immediately The Fox threw back his woolen blanket which was ornamented on the inside with more than two hundred small decorative designs of horses. Among the Pawnees, and likewise, if I remember rightly, among the Otoes and Omahas, robes and blankets were thus embellished and so made to pass current as real certificates of a choice brand of character for their wearers. Each horse depicted on the robe was notice that the owner and wearer had stolen such horse. Finally, after expressions of friendship and good will, the expedition in charge of The Fox bade us adieu and briskly walked southward on their mission for getting horses away from their traditional enemies.

It is perhaps worth while to mention that, it being in the autumn of the year, all these Indians were carefully and deftly arrayed in autumn-colored costumes. Their blankets, head-gear, and everything else were the color of dead and dried prairie grass. This disguise was for the purpose of making themselves as nearly indistinguishable as possible on the brown surface of the far-stretching plains. For then the weeds and grasses had all been bleached by the fall frosts. We were given an exhibition of the nearly perfect invisibleness of The Fox by his taking a position near a badger hole around which a lot of tall weeds had grown upon the prairie, and really the almost exact similitude of coloring which he had cunningly reproduced in his raiment made him even at a short distance indistinguishable among the faded weeds and grasses by which he was surrounded.

In due time we reached Fort Kearny and after a pleasant and most agreeable visit with Mr. Heth and his family, Colonel Alexander and Lieutenant Bush, I pushed on alone for the Missouri river, by the North Platte route, bringing home with me two or three turkeys and a quarter of buffalo meat.

About the second evening, as I remember it, I arrived at the agency of the four bands of the Pawnee on the Loup fork of the Platte river, near where the village of Genoa in Nance county now stands. Judge Gillis of Pennsylvania was the U. S. government agent then in charge of that tribe, and Mr. Allis was his interpreter. There I experienced the satisfaction of going leisurely and observingly through the villages of the four bands of Pawnees, which there made their habitation. The names of the four confederate bands of Pawnee Indians were Grand Pawnee, Wolf Pawnee, Republican Pawnee, and Tapage Pawnee. At that time, they all together numbered between four thousand and five thousand.

Distinguished among them for fearlessness and impetuous courage and constant success in war was an Indian who had been born with his left hand so shrunken and shriveled that it looked like the contracted claw of a bird. He was celebrated among all the tribes of the plains as "Crooked Hand, the Fighter." Hearing me express a wish for making the acquaintance of this famous warrior and scalp accumulator, Judge Gillis and Mr. Allis kindly volunteered to escort me to his domicile and formally introduce me. We took the trail which lay across Beaver creek up into the village. This village was composed of very large, earthen, mound-like wigwams. From a distance they looked like a number of great kettles turned wrong side up on the prairie. Finally, we came to the entrance of the abode of Crooked Hand. He was at home. I was presented to him by the interpreter, Mr. Allis. Through him, addressing the tawny hero who stood before me, I said:

It has come to my ears that you are and always have been a very brave man in battle. Therefore, I have made a long journey to see you and to shake the hand of a great warrior.

This seemed to suit his bellicose eminence and to appeal to his barbaric vanity. Consequently, I continued, saying: I hear that you have skillfully killed a great many Sioux and that you have kept the scalp of each warrior slain by you. If this be true, I wish you would show me these trophies of your courage and victories?

148

Immediately Crooked Hand reached under a sort of rude settee and pulled out a very cheap traveling trunk, which was locked. Then taking a string from around his neck he found the key thereunto attached, inserted it in the lock, turned it, and with gloating satisfaction threw back the lid of the trunk. It is fair to state that, notwithstanding Mr. Crooked Hand's personal adornments in the way of paint, earrings, and battle mementoes, he was evidently not a man of much personal property, for the trunk contained not one other portable thing except a string of thirteen scalps. This he lifted out with his right hand and held up before me as a connoisseur would exhibit a beautiful cameo—with intense satisfaction and self-praise expressed in his features.

The scalps were not large, averaging not much more in circumference than a silver dollar (before the crime of 1873). Each scalp was big enough to firmly and gracefully retain the scalp-lock which its original possessor had nourished. Each scalp was neatly lined with flaming red flannel and encircled by and stitched to a willow twig just as boys so stretch and preserve squirrel skins. Then there was a strong twine which ran through the center of each of the thirteen scalps leaving a space of something like three or four inches between each two.

After looking at these ghastly certificates of prowess in Indian warfare I said to the possessor: "Do you still like to go into fights with the Sioux?" He replied hesitatingly:

"Yes, I go into the fights with the Sioux, but I stay only until I can kill one man, get his scalp and get out of the battle."

Then I asked: "Why do you do this way now, and so act differently from the fighting plans of your earlier years when you remained to the end of the conflict?" Instantly he replied and gave me this aboriginal explanation:

"You see, my friend, I have only one life. To me death must come only once. But I have taken thirteen lives. And now when I go into battle there are thirteen chances of my being killed to one of my coming out of the fight alive."

149

This aboriginal application of the doctrine of chance is equally as reasonable as some of the propositions relating to chances found in "Hedges' Logic," which I studied in the regular college course. There is more excuse for a savage faith in chance than can be made for the superstitious belief in it which is held by some civilized people.

My last buffalo hunt was finished, and its trophies and its choicest memories safely stored for exhibition or reminiscence at Arbor Lodge. More than thirty-seven years afterwards I am permitted this evening by your indulgence and consideration to attempt faintly to portray the country and its primitive condition at that time in that particular section of Nebraska which is now Franklin county.

But in concluding this discursive and desultory narrative I cannot refrain from referring to, and briefly descanting on, another and an earlier and larger expedition into the valley of the Republican which set out from Mexico in the year 1540 under the command of Coronado.

That explorer was undoubtedly the first white man to visit Nebraska. In his report to the Spanish government is a description of buffalo which for graphic minuteness and correctness has never been excelled. Thus, it pictures them as they appeared to him and his followers more than three hundred and fifty years ago:

"These oxen are of the bigness and color of our bulls, but their horns are not so great. They have a great bunch upon their foreshoulders, and more hair upon their fore-part than on their hinder-part; and it is like wool. They have, as it were, a horse mane upon their backbone, and much hair, and very long from the knees downward. They have great tufts of hair hanging down their foreheads, and it seemeth they have beards, because of the great store of hair hanging down at their chins and throats. The males have very long tails, and a great knob or flock at the end, so that in some respects they resemble the lion, and in some other the camel. They push with their horns, they run, they overtake and kill a horse when they are in their rage and anger. Finally, it is a fierce beast of countenance and form of body. The horses fled from them, either because of their deformed shape, or because they had never seen them before. Their masters [meaning no doubt the Indians] have no other riches or substance; of them they eat, they drink, they apparel, they shoe themselves; and of their hides they make many things, as houses, shoes, apparel and robes; of their bones they make bodkins; of their sinews and hair, thread; of their horns, maws and bladders, vessels; of their dung, fire; and of their calf skins, budgets, wherein they draw and keep water. To be short, they make so many things of them as they have need of, or as may suffice them in the use of this life."

It is perhaps a work of supererogation for me after the lapse of three and a half centuries to endorse and verify the accuracy of that word picture of the buffalo. A photograph of the great herd which I rode into during my hunt could hardly better convey to the mind the images of buffalo. The hundreds of years intervening between my own excursion into the valley of the Republican and the invasion of Coronado had neither impaired, improved, nor perceptibly changed either the buffalo or the soil of that fertile section now comprising the county of Franklin in the state of Nebraska. Of that immediate propinquity Coronado said: "The place I have reached is in the fortieth degree of latitude. The earth is the best possible for all kinds of productions of Spain, for while it is very strong and black, it is very well watered by brooks, springs, and rivers. I found prunes" [wild plums, no doubt, just as my party and the wild turkeys were feasting upon in October, 1861] "like those of Spain, some of which are black; also some excellent grapes and mulberries."

And Jaramillo, who was with Coronado, says: "This country has a superb appearance, and such that I have not seen better in all Spain, neither in Italy nor France, nor in any other country where I have been in the service of your majesty. It is not a country of mountains; there are only some hills, some plains and some streams of very fine water. It satisfies me completely. I presume that it is very fertile and favorable for the cultivation of all kinds of fruits."

And this land whence the Coronado expedition upon foot retraced its march to Old Mexico, a distance, by the trail he made, of 3,230 miles, was in latitude forty degrees and distant westward from the Missouri about one hundred and forty miles. Geographically, topographically, and in every other way, the description of Franklin and the neighborhood of Riverton in that county.

Here then in Franklin county it is recorded that the last horse belonging to Coronado and his band of precious-metal hunters died. At that time, all the horses on this continent had been imported. The loss of this animal that day at that place was like the loss today of a man-of-war for Spain in a great naval conflict with the United States. It was discouraging and overwhelming and resulted in the relinquishment of further exploration for the land of Quivera—the home of gold and silver—and the return to Old Mexico. There was no use for saddles, bridles and other equestrian trappings, for with no horse to ride even stirrups were thrown away, and it has been the good fortune of Nebraska to have them exhumed after a sequestration of more than three centuries.

And thus, after so many years of delay, I give you the story of the first buffalo hunt and the last buffalo hunt in the Republican Valley concerning which I am competent to make statement.

Notable Nebraskan, Julius Sterling Morton was born April 22, 1832 in Adams, New York. Morton, along with Robert Furnas, was the co-founder of Arbor Day.

After finishing school at the University of Michigan, Morton married his school sweetheart, Caroline ("Carrie") Joy French in 1854. They left for the Nebraska Territory on the day of their marriage.

Morton and his wife, Carrie, settled in Nebraska City where he became the editor of the Nebraska News. His life-long interest in writing and publishing had begun in his grandfather's newspaper office in Michigan.

During the years between 1867-1882, Morton dropped out of politics in order to spend more time promoting agriculture. He served on the Nebraska State Board of Agriculture and was a member of the state's Horticultural Society. He supported better farming methods, conservation programs, and tree planting.

In 1872 the Nebraska State Board of Agriculture adopted Morton's resolution to create Arbor Day, a day set aside to plant trees. Prizes were offered to counties and individuals for planting properly the largest number of trees on that day. It was estimated that more than one million trees were planted in Nebraska on the first Arbor Day.

Nebraska celebrates Arbor Day on the last Friday of April. All 50 states celebrate this holiday, although the dates may vary to match each local climate's best time to plant trees.

Morton died in 1902 at his son's home in Illinois. J. Sterling Morton was inducted into the Nebraska Hall of Fame in 1975-76.[15]

---

[15] https://nebraskastudies.org/en/1850-1874/j-sterling-morton-founder-of-arbor-day/

HOW THE FOUNDER OF ARBOR DAY CREATED THE MOST FAMOUS WESTERN ESTATE

BY PAUL MORTON

"The memories that live and bloom in trees, that whisper of the loved and lost in summer leaves, are as imperishable as the seasons of the year—immortal as the love of a mother."—J. STERLING MORTON.

I suppose the story of a successful pioneer will always interest and encourage people. The narrative of a strong, far-sighted man who makes something out of nothing seems to put heart into the average worker. That is why I am telling the story of how my father, J. Sterling Morton, and his young wife, set their faces toward the West, one October day in 1854, and built them a home on the prairies.

Arbor Lodge as it stands today, with its classic porticoes, its gardens, and its arboretum, the present country home of my brother, Mr. Joy Morton, is not the home that I remember as a boy. That was a much more modest edifice. Yet even that house was a palace compared with the first one, which was a little log-cabin standing on the lonely prairie, exposed to blizzards and Indians, and with scarcely a tree in sight.

My father was a young newspaper man in Detroit, only recently out of college, when he took his bride, two years his junior, out to the little-known frontier. Attracted by the information about the new country brought out by Douglas and others in the Kansas-Nebraska debates in congress, he conceived and acted on the idea that here were fortunes to be made. Taking such household goods as they could, they traveled to the new land, making the last stage up the Missouri river by boat.

Nebraska at that time was the Indian's own country. There were not over 1,500 white people in the entire state. All the country west of the Missouri was called in the geographies the Great American Desert, and it took a good deal of faith to believe that anything could be made to grow where annual fires destroyed even the prairie grass and the fringes of cottonwoods and scrub-oaks along the rivers. Today this section, within a radius of some two hundred miles, includes perhaps the most fertile soil in the world and has become a center of industry, agriculture, and horticulture for the middle west. There was then no political organization, no laws; men went about fully armed. There were no roads and no bridges to speak of in the entire state; it was "waste land."

This was part of the land of the Louisiana Purchase, and my father bought a quarter section (160 acres) from the man who preempted it from the government. The price paid was $1.25 an acre. Today the estate comprises about 1,000 acres, and the land is readily saleable at a hundred times this price.

On the spot where Arbor Lodge now stands, my father built his first log-cabin. This was soon replaced by a modest frame house; there was not then another frame house between it and the Rocky Mountains, six hundred miles away. On the same place two succeeding houses were built by my father, the present, and fifth, Arbor Lodge having been built by his sons after his death. My father called these first four houses, "seed, bud, blossom, and fruit."

155

The first winter was a mild one, fortunately, but there were plenty of hardships for the young people. There were no very near neighbors, the village of Kearny Heights, now Nebraska City, being then over two miles away. The Indians formed the greatest danger. I can remember a day in my boyhood when we had everything packed up, ready to flee across the Missouri to Iowa from the murderous Pawnees and Cheyennes, who, fortunately, did not come that time. A part of that first winter my father and mother spent in Bellevue.

When spring came, they set about building their home. Later on, they had young trees sent to them from the East, including some excellent varieties of apples, peaches, cherries, pears, etc. Things grew fast; it was only the prairie fires that had kept the land a desert so long, and year by year these fires had enriched the soil.

The farm was located on the Overland trail, the favorite route to Pike's Peak and the El Dorado. Many of the Mormon emigrants crossed the river at that place. I can remember the big trains of ox and mule teams passing the house.

My father's interests were always inseparably joined with those of the community; he was in public life from the start, and Nebraska's fortunes were his. His neighbors all had the same experiences, and many a farmer who started with nothing is now wealthy. The farmers had to bring in from Missouri and Iowa all the food for themselves and their horses and cattle the first year. They were living on faith. During the first spring and summer the anxiety was great, but they were rewarded by a good harvest in the fall. The success of that harvest settled the Nebraska question forever. It was a land that could support its inhabitants.

But the end was not yet. The "get-rich-quick" fever struck the community. Immigration was over-stimulated, and town lots were manufactured at a great rate. In a few months they increased in price from $300 to $3,000 apiece. Banks were created and money was made plenty by legislation. My father never caught this fever, being always a sound-money man and believing in wealth based on the soil.

156

At the end of the second summer the crop of town lots and Nebraska bank-notes was greater than the crop of corn. But the lesson was not learned until the panic of 1857 drove out the speculators and left the farmers in possession of the territory. With the spring of 1858 sanity came to rule once more, and there was less bank making and more prairie breaking. The citizens had learned that agriculture was to be the salvation of the new country. In 1857, two dollars a bushel had been paid for imported corn, but in 1859 the same steamers that had brought it in bore thousands of bushels south at forty cents a bushel, bringing more money into the territory than all the sales of town lots for a year.

The first territorial fair was held in Nebraska City in 1859, and on that occasion my father made a speech in which he reviewed the history of the new territory up to that time. I speak of these things because my father was always a man of public interests, and his fortunes were wrapped up in those of the territory. His hardships came when the community went crazy, and his fortune grew when sanity was once more restored.

I know of nothing that better illustrates my father's private character than an editorial which he wrote and published in *The Conservative* a short time before the untimely death of my brother Carl. The fact that both the author and the two loved ones of whom he so tenderly wrote have passed to the Great Beyond, imparts to this beautiful passage a most exquisite pathos:

"It was a bright, balmy morning in April, more than a quarter of a century ago. The sun was nursing the young grass into verdure, and the prairie was just beginning to put off its winter coat of somber colorings. Tranquil skies and morning mists were redolent at Arbor Lodge of the coming resurrection of the foliage and flowers that died the autumn before. All about the cottage home there was hope and peace; and everywhere the signs of woman's watchful love and tidy care, when, suddenly, toned with affectionate solicitude, rang out: 'Carl, Carl!' but no answer came. Downstairs, upstairs, at the barn, even in the well, everywhere, the mother's voice called anxiously, again and again. But the silence, menacing and frightening, was unbroken by an answer from the lost boy. At last, however, he was found behind a smokehouse, busily digging in the ground with a small spade, though only five years of age, and he said: 'I'm too busy to talk. I'm planting an orchard,' and sure enough, he had set out a seedling apple tree, a small cottonwood, and a little elm.

"The delighted mother clasped him in her arms, kissed him, and said: 'This orchard must not be destroyed.'

"And so now

"'I hear the muffled tramp of years
Come stealing up the slopes of Time;
They bear a train of smiles and tears
Of burning hopes and dreams sublime.'

"The child's orchard is more than thirty years of age. The cottonwood is a giant now, and its vibrant foliage talks, summer after summer, in the evening breeze with humanlike voice, and tells its life story to the graceful, swaying elm near by, while the gnarled and scrubby little apple tree, shaped, as to its head, like a despondent toadstool, stands in dual shade, and bears small sweet apples, year after year, in all humility. But that orchard must not be destroyed. It was established by the youngest tree planter who ever planted in this tree planter's state, and for his sake and the memory of the sweet soul who nursed and loved him, it lives and grows, one cottonwood, one apple tree, one elm.

"'But O, for the touch of a vanished hand,
And the sound of a voice that is still.

"The memories that live and bloom in trees, that whisper of the loved and lost in summer leaves, are as imperishable as the seasons of the year—immortal as the love of a mother."

158

EARLY REMINISCENCES OF NEBRASKA CITY

BY ELLEN KINNEY WARE

Social Aspects

As a girl graduate, I came to Nebraska City from Virginia, at an early day. It seemed to me that I was leaving everything attractive socially and intellectually behind me, but I was mistaken. On arriving here, I expected to see quite a town, was disappointed, for two large brick hotels, and a few scattered houses comprised the place. Among my first acquaintances was the family of Governor Black, consisting of his daughter about my own age, his wife, and himself. He was not only bright and clever, but a wit as well, and famous as a story-teller. Alas a sad fate awaited him. For leaving here to take command of a Pennsylvania regiment, he was killed early in the civil war.

Those were freighting days and Russell, Majors and Waddell, government freighters, made this their headquarters. Alexander Majors brought his family here adding much socially to the town. Major Martin, an army officer, was stationed here. He was a charming gentleman and had a lovely wife. Dancing was the principal amusement with the young people. Informal dances at private homes and occasionally on a steamboat when it arrived, brilliantly lighted and having a band of music on board. At the "Outfit" as it was called, where the supplies for the freighting company were kept, dwelt a family, Raisin by name, who were exceedingly hospitable, not only entertaining frequently, but often sending an ambulance for their guests. At these parties, no round dancing was indulged in, just simple quadrilles and the lancers. Mr. and Mrs. J. Sterling Morton, who lived on a country place, a short distance from town, which has since become widely known as Arbor Lodge, were among the most active entertainers, dispensing that delightful hospitality for which in later times they were so well known.

And so, we lived without railroads, without telephones, automobiles, or theaters. But I believe that our social enjoyment was greater than it is now. Instead of railroads, we had steam boats arriving almost daily from St. Louis, St. Joseph, and other towns. In carriages we drove to Omaha and back, and the social intercourse of the two towns was much greater than it is now.

Amateur theatricals took the place of the theater, and often brilliant, undreamed of talent was shown. Literature also was not neglected; many highly educated men and women were among our pioneers and literary societies were a prominent part of our social life. We played chess in those days, but not cards. This alone might be taken as an index of how much less frivolous that day was than the present.

In 1860 Bishop Talbot arrived here from Indianapolis and made this his home, adding greatly socially and intellectually to the life of the community. In his family was the Rev. Isaac Hager, beloved and revered by all who knew him, a most thorough musician, as well as a fine preacher.

Remembering old times, we sometimes ask ourselves, where now are the men and women, equal to the ones we knew in those days, certainly there are none superior to them, in intellect, manners, wit, and true nobility.

"Oh, brave hearts journeyed to the west,
When this old town was new!"

Ellen Kinney Ware was born at Mount Vernon, Ohio, on July 25, 1841. Mrs. Ware was educated in the private schools of the south, and was graduated with honors from Virginia Female Institute, now called Stewart's Hall, in 1858. Since that date she has lived in Nebraska with the exception of several winters spent in California. She has always been an enthusiastic admirer of Nebraska and has written articles on the early history of the state and various biographical papers for numerous societies and newspapers.

Her marriage to Jasper Anderson Ware was solemnized on October 10, 1861. Mr. Ware, who was born at Trenton, KY, March 5, 1831, was a merchant, broker, and banker. He was the son of Edmond and Louisa Virginia (Anderson) Ware and was descended from Nicholas Merriweather. Major Anderson of Fort Sumpter fame was also an ancestor. He died at Nebraska City, November 20, 1900. Four children were born to this union.

Mrs. Ware [was] a charger member of the Daughters of the American Revolution, Otoe Chapter, and during the World War was active in the work of the Red Cross. She [was] vitally interested in child welfare; [was] a member of the Associated Charities; and [was] active in Women's Club work. She [was] a member of the St. Mary's Episcopal Church at Nebraska City, where she always took part in all church affairs.[16]

16

http://www.usgennet.org/usa/ne/topic/resources/OLLibrary/Nebraskana/page s/nbka0275.htm

SOME PERSONAL INCIDENTS

BY W. A. MCALLISTER

My father and family came to Nebraska in 1858, living two years at Genoa. At this time, the government assigned what is now Nance county, to the Pawnee Indians, as a reservation. When the white settlers sought other homes, our family located eight miles east of Columbus, at McAllister's lake. Every fall my father hired about sixty squaws to husk out his crop of corn. Only one buck ever came to work, and he was always known as "Squaw Charlie" after that. He spoke English quite well. They were slow workers, husking about twenty bushels per day. They were very gluttonous at meals, eating much bread, with meat soup containing potatoes and other vegetables, cooked in large twenty gallon camp kettles. This was supplemented by watermelons by the wagonload. It required a week or ten days to harvest the corn crop. The Indians were very thievish, stealing almost as much as their wages amounted to. During these years I often witnessed their "Medicine Dances."

When fifteen years old I enlisted in Company B, Second Nebraska Cavalry, and went to Fort Kearny. Our company relieved the Tenth Infantry, which went to the front. In less than twenty days this company was nearly annihilated at the battle of Fredericksburg.

163

While at the fort a buffalo hunt was organized by the officers, and I had an opportunity to go. Our party went south to the valley of the Republican. The first night we camped at the head of the Big Blue, and the second day I noticed south of us, about eight miles distant, a dark line along the horizon extending as far east and west as the eye could reach. I inquired what it was, and an old hunter replied "buffaloes." I could not believe him, but in a few hours found he was right, for we were surrounded by millions of them. They were hurrying to the east with a roaring like distant thunder. Our sportsmen moved in a body through the herd looking for calves, not caring to carry back the meat of the old specimens. Strange to say this tremendous herd seemed to be composed of males, for the cows were still on the Oklahoma ranges caring for their calves, until strong enough to tramp north again. We noticed an old fellow making good progress on three legs, one foot having been injured. One of the party wished to dispose of him, but his wooly forehead covered with sand, turned every bullet. Finally, the hunter asked me to attract his attention, while he placed a bullet in his heart. In doing this, he almost succeeded in goring my pony, but I turned a second too quickly for him. I was near enough to see the fire flashing from his angry eyes. In a few minutes he fell with a thud.

Several years after the war being over, I worked for the Union Pacific railroad company. At Kearney, in 1869, we met the Buck surveying party, who had come west to lay out, for the government, the lands of the Republican Valley. In this company was a young man from Pontiac, Illinois, named Harry McGregor. He left a home of plenty to hunt buffalo and Indians, but found among other privations, he could not have all the sugar he wished, so at Kearney he decided to leave the party and work with us. This decision saved his life, for the rest of the surveyors, about ten in all, after starting south next morning, were never seen again. They were surprised and killed by the Indians. Their skeletons were found several years later, bleaching on the Nebraska prairie.

MAJOR NORTH'S BUFFALO HUNT

BY MINNIE FREEMAN PENNY

A party under the direction of Major Frank North set out with six wagon teams and four buffalo horses on November 13, 1871, to engage in a buffalo hunt. The other men were Luther North, C. Stanley, Hopkins Brown, Charles Freeman, W. E. Freeman, W. E. Freeman, Jr., and Messrs. Bonesteel, Wasson, and Cook. They camped the first night at James Cushing's ranch, eighteen miles out; the second night at Jason Parker's home at Lone Tree, now Central City, and the third night arrived at Grand Island. On the way to Grand Island one of the party accidentally started a prairie fire six miles east of Grand Island. A hard fight was made, and the flames subdued just in time to save a settler's stable.

Leaving Grand Island on the sixteenth they crossed the Platte river and camped on the West Blue. From this point in the journey the party suffered incredible hardships until their return.

About midnight the wind changed to the north, bringing rain and sleet, and inside of an hour a blizzard was raging on the open prairie. The horses were covered with snow and ice and there was no fuel for the fires. The men went out as far as they dared to go for wood, being unsuccessful. It was decided to try to follow the Indian trail south—made by the Pawnee scouts under Major North. Little progress could be made and they soon "struck camp" near some willows that afforded a little protection to their horses and a "windbreak" was made for man and beast. This camp was at the head of the Big Sandy, called by this party the "Big Smoky" for the men suffered agonies from the smoke in the little tipi.

For two days the storm continued in all its terrible force. The wind blew and the air was so full of snow that it was blinding. The cold was intense. The men finally determined to find some habitation at any price and in groups of two and three left camp following the creek where they were sure some one had settled. A sod house was found occupied by two English families who received the party most hospitably. Charles Freeman, older than the other men of the party, suffered a collapse and remained at this home. During the night, the storm abated and next morning, finding all the ravines choked with heavy snow drifts, it was decided by vote to abandon the hunt. They dug out their belongings from under many feet of snow, sold their corn to the English families to lighten their load and started back. The journey home was full of accidents, bad roads, and drifted ravines. Reaching the Union Pacific railroad at Grand Island Major North and Mr. Bonesteel returned to Columbus by rail, also Mr. Stanley from Lone Tree. The rest of the party returned by team, arriving on November 24.

Major North admitted that of all his experiences on the prairie—not excepting his years with the Pawnee scouts—this "beat them all" as hazardous and perplexing.

The foregoing is taken from my father's diary.

PIONEER LIFE

BY MRS. JAMES G. REEDER

It is almost impossible for people of the present day to realize the hardships and privations that the first settlers in Nebraska underwent. Imagine coming to a place where there was nothing but what you had brought with you in wagons. Add to the discomfort of being without things which in your former home had seemed necessities, the pests which abound in a new country: the rattlesnake, the coyote, the skunk, the weasel, and last—but not least—the flea.

My father, Samuel C. Smith, held the post of "trader" for the Pawnee Indians under Major Wheeler in 1865-66. We lived in a house provided by the government, near the Indian school at Genoa, or "The Reservation," as it was commonly called. I was only a few weeks old, and in order to keep me away from the fleas, a torture to everyone, they kept me in a shallow basket of Indian weave, suspended from the ceiling by broad bands of webbing, far enough from the floor and wall to insure safety.

I have heard my mother tell of how the Indians would walk right into the house without knocking, or press their faces against a window and peer in. They were usually respectful; they simply knew no better. Sometimes in cold weather three or four big men

167

would walk into the kitchen and insist upon staying by the fire, and mother would have hard work to drive them out.

The next year my father moved his family to a homestead two miles east of Genoa where he had built a large log house and stables surrounded by a high tight fence, which was built for protection against the unfriendly Indians who frequently came to make war on the Pawnees. The government at times kept a company of soldiers stationed just north of us, and when there would be an "Indian scare," the officers' wives as well as our few neighbors would come to our place for safety. Major Noyes was at one time stationed there. Firearms of all sorts were always kept handy, and my mother could use them as skillfully as my father.

One night my father's barn was robbed of eight horses by the Sioux and the same band took ten head from Mr. Gerrard, who lived four miles east of us. E. A. Gerrard, Luther North, and my father followed their trail to the Missouri river opposite Yankton, South Dakota, and did not see a white man while they were gone. They did not recover the horses, but twenty years after the government paid the original cost of the horses without interest. The loss of these horses and the accidental death of a brother of mine so discouraged my father that he moved to Columbus in 1870.

One of the delights of my childhood were the nights in early autumn when all the neighborhood would go out to burn the grass from the prairie north of us for protection against "prairie fires," as great a foe as was the unfriendly Indian of a few years before.

In the summer of 1874, which in Nebraska history is known as "the grasshopper year," my grandmother, Mrs. William Boone, accompanied by her daughter, Mrs. Mary Hemphill, and granddaughter, Ada Hemphill, came to make us a visit. For their entertainment we drove in a three-seated platform spring wagon or carryall to see the Indians in their village near Genoa. Their lodges were made of earth in a circular form with a long narrow entrance extending out like the handle of a frying pan. As we neared the village we came upon an ordinary looking Indian walking in the road, and to our surprise my father greeted him very cordially and introduced him to us. It was Petalesharo, chief of the Pawnees, but without the feathers and war-paint that I imagined a chief would always wear. He invited us to his lodge, and we drove to the entrance, but my grandmother and aunt could not be persuaded to leave the surrey. My cousin, being more venturesome, started in with my father, but had gone only a few steps when she gathered up her skirts and cried, "Oh, look at the fleas! Just see them hop!" and came running back to the rig, assuring us she had seen enough. The Indians must have taken the fleas with them when they moved to Oklahoma, for we seldom see one now.

Samuel Church Smith was born July 10, 1825, in Haddam, Connecticut. In 1859 he was married to Clara A. Boone, a great-niece of the Kentucky scout, Daniel Boone.

Mr. Smith, a resident of Platte County for twenty-one years, came here in 1865 to take charge of a government trading post on the Pawnee Indian Reservation at Genoa. He remained there for one year. Then for four years following, he occupied a farm in the Looking Glass Valley. In 1870 he moved to Columbus where he lived for sixteen years. He was in the real estate business, which kept him in close touch with all the early homesteaders. Mr. Smith was never a public man, but he left the record of being very progressive and public spirited man. He was liberal with his money and energy and thereby encouraged public improvements and enterprises.

He and Clara had three children: Elmer, George, and Lillian (Mrs. James G. Reeder of Columbus), Elmer, a civil engineer, who was one of the first to go to the Panama Canal Zone. He worked on the Nicaraguan Survey and did preliminary work on the Isthmus. He did some of the most important work in the Canal Zone. He had patented a device to be used in the construction of the dams which attracted wide attention in engineering circles. Elmer Church Smith died July 10, 1906, in the Canal Zone, of malaria.

George Boone Smith, born in Clarksville, Missouri, spent his early life there and learned the printer's trade and gave much time to the study of music. He was in the real estate business for twelve years with his father in San Diego. Later he was with the National City Newspaper in National City. He was married to Mary Alice Morrell, whom he met in the newspaper business. They had one son, Clarence Smith.

Clara Boone Smith died May 27, 1886, and in that year, Mr. Smith moved to California. In 1887 he married Louisa Lehman of Des Moines, Iowa, a sister of George Lehman, of Columbus. Mr. Smith died in 1907.[17]

EARLY DAYS IN POLK COUNTY

BY CALMAR McCUNE

In the early history of the county, county warrants were thicker than the leaves on the trees (for trees were scarce then), and of money in the pockets of most people there was none. Those were the days when that genial plutocrat, William H. Waters, relieved the necessities of the needy by buying up county warrants for seventy-five cents on the dollar. Don't understand this as a reflection on the benevolent intentions of Mr. Waters, for he paid as high a price as anybody else offered; I mention it only to illustrate the financial condition of the people and the body politic.

Henry Mahan was postmaster and general merchant. The combined post office and store which, with a blacksmith shop, constituted the business part of the town of Osceola, was located on the west side of the square. It was a one and one-half story frame and on the second floor was *The Homesteader* (now the Osceola *Record*). Here H. T. Arnold, W. F. Kimmel, Frank Burgess, the writer, and Stephen Fleharty exercised their gray matter by grinding out of their exuberant and sometimes lurid imaginations original local items and weighty editorials. In those days if a top buggy was seen out on the open, treeless prairie, the entire business population turned out to watch it and soon there were bets as to whether it came from Columbus or Seward, for then there was not a top buggy in Polk county. The first drug store was opened by John Beltzer, a country blacksmith who suddenly blossomed from the anvil into a full-fledged pharmacist. Doctor Stone compounded the important prescriptions for a while.

I need not try to describe the grasshopper raid of 1874 for the old-timers remember it and I could not picture the tragedy so that others could see it. To see the sun's rays dimmed by the flying agents of destruction; to witness the disappearance of every vestige of green vegetation—the result of a year's labor, which was to most of the inhabitants the only resource against actual want, to see this I say, one must live through it. Many of the early settlers were young people newly married, who had left their homes in the East with all their earthly possessions in a covered wagon, or "prairie schooner" as it was called, and making the trip overland, had landed with barely enough money to exist until the first crop was harvested. Added to the loss and privation entailed by the visitation of the winged host was the constant dread that the next season would bring a like scourge.

On Sunday afternoon, April 13, 1873, I left the farm home of James Bell in Valley precinct for Columbus, expecting to take the train there Monday morning for Omaha. The season was well advanced, the treeless prairie being covered with verdure. It was a balmy sunshiny spring day, as nearly ideal as even Nebraska can produce.

As I left the Clother hotel that evening to attend the Congregational church I noticed that the clouds were banking heavily in the northwest. There was a roll of distant thunder, a flash of lightning, and a series of gentle spring showers followed and it was raining when I went to bed at my hotel. Next morning when I looked out of my window, I could not see half-way across the street. The wind was blowing a gale, which drove large masses of large, heavy snow-flakes southward. Already where obstructions were met the huge drifts were forming. This continued without cessation of either snow or wind all day Monday and until late Tuesday night. Wednesday about noon the snow plow came, followed by the Monday train, which I boarded for Omaha. As the train neared Fremont, I could see the green

172

knolls peeping up through the snow, and at Omaha the snow had disappeared. There they had had mainly rain instead of snow. I may say that the storm area was not over two hundred miles wide with Clarks as about the center, the volume gradually diminishing each way from that point. It should be borne in mind that the farmers raised mainly spring wheat and oats. These grains had been sown several weeks before the storm and were all up, but the storm did not injure them in the least.

On leaving Omaha a few days later I went to Grand Island. At Gardner's Siding, between Columbus and Clarks, a creek passed under the track. This had filled bank high with snow which now melting, formed a lake. The track being bad the train ran so slowly that I had time to count fifty floating carcasses of cattle upon the surface of the water. This was the fate of many thousands of head of stock.

Nobody dared to venture out into that storm for no human being could face it and live. The great flakes driven by a fifty-mile gale would soon plaster shut eyes, nose, and mouth—in fact, so swift was the gale that no headway could be made against it.

In those days merchants hauled their goods from Columbus or Seward and all the grain marketed went to the same points. Wheat only was hauled; corn being used for feed or fuel.

A trip to Columbus and return the same day meant something. A start while the stars still twinkled; the mercury ten, twenty, or even thirty degrees below, was not a pleasure trip, to the driver on a load of wheat. But the driver was soon compelled to drop from the seat, and trudge along slapping his hands and arms against his body to keep from freezing. Leaving home at three or four o'clock in the morning he was lucky if he got home again, half frozen and very weary, several hours after dark. Speaking of exposure to wintry blasts, reminds me of a trip on foot I made shortly after my arrival in Polk county. December 24, 1872, I started to walk from the Milsap neighborhood in Hamilton county, several miles west of where Polk now stands, to the home of William Stevens, near the schoolhouse of District No. 5. It was a clear, bitter cold

173

morning, the wind blowing strongly from the northwest, the ground coated with a hard crust of snow. I kept my bearings as best I could, for it should be remembered that there were no roads or landmarks, and I was traveling purely by guess. Along about mid-day I stumbled upon a little dugout, somewhere north of where Stromsburg now stands—the first house I had seen. On entering I found a young couple who smiled me a welcome, which was the best they could do, for, as I saw from the inscriptions on a couple of boxes, they were recent arrivals from Sweden. The young lady gave me some coffee and rusks, and I am bound to say that I never tasted better food than that coffee and those rusks. I did not see another house until I reached the bluffs, where, about sunset, I was gladdened by the sight of the Stevens house in the valley, a couple of miles distant. When I finally reached this hospitable home the fingers of both hands were frozen and my nose and ears badly frosted.

In the early days we traveled from point to point by the nearest and most direct route, for while the land was being rapidly taken up, there were no section line roads. Whenever the contour of the land permitted, we angled, being careful to avoid the patches of cultivated land. There were no trees, no fences, and very few buildings, so, on the level prairie, nothing obstructed the view as far as the eye could carry. The sod houses and stables were a godsend, for lumber was very expensive and most of the settlers brought with them lean purses. It required no high-priced, skilled labor to build a "soddy," and properly built they were quite comfortable.

When I grow reminiscent and allow my mind to go back to those pioneer days, the span of time between then and now seems very brief, but when I think longer and compare the *then* with the *now*, it seems as though that sod house-treeless-ox driving period must have been at least one hundred years ago. It is a far cry from the ox team to the automobile.

Calmar McCune, editor of the Osceola Record, was born in Pittsburgh, Penn, February 15, 1849. At the age of twelve years he went to West Virginia with his parents, where he lived until the breaking-out of the war. He enlisted in

Company K, First Maryland Volunteer Cavalry, in 1864, being only sixteen years old, and served until the close of the war, after which he went to Mount Vernon, Iowa, where he entered Cornell College, being a student there for four years, and then became city editor of the daily paper at Cedar Rapids, continuing there for one year, and in 1872 went to Marion, Iowa, and established the paper now known as the Marion Liberal.

This he edited but a short time and in the winter of the same year, removed to Nebraska, and in the spring of 1873, took up a homestead in the Osceola Precinct. In the spring of 1874, he edited the Homesteader at Osceola for one year, and in the fall of 1877 went do David City, Butler County. There he established the David City Republican, which he ran until April 1880, at that time going into the real estate and abstract business. After pursuing this for a short time, he went to Florida, returning from there to Osceola in the spring of 1881.

Mr. McCune was married in August 1873 to Miss Julia Bell, by whom he has four children, three girls and one boy.[18]

---

[18] https://www.findagrave.com/memorial/31383147/calmar-mccune

PERSONAL REMINISCENCES

BY MRS. THYRZA REAVIS ROY

In March 1865, my husband, George Roy, and I started from our home in Avon, Illinois, to Nebraska territory. The railroad extended to St. Joseph, Missouri. There they told us we would have to take a steamboat up the Missouri river to Rulo, forty miles from St. Joseph. We took passage on a small steamboat, but the ice was breaking up and the boat ran only four miles up the river. They said it was too dangerous to go farther so told us we would have to go back or land and get some one to drive us to Rulo, or the Missouri side of the river across from Rulo. We decided to land and hired a man to drive us across country in an old wagon. It was very cold and when we reached the place where we would have to cross the Missouri, the ice was running in immense blocks. It was sunset, we were forty miles from a house on that side of the river. There was a man on the other side of the river in a small skiff. Mr. Roy waved to him and he crossed and took us in. Every moment it seemed those cakes of ice would crush the little skiff, but the man was an expert dodger and after a perilous ride he let us off at Rulo. By that time, it was dark. We went to a roughly boarded up shanty they called a tavern. It snowed that night and the snow beat in on our bed. The next morning, we hired a man to take us to Falls City, ten miles from Rulo. Falls City was a hamlet of scarcely three hundred souls. There was a log cabin on the square; one tiny schoolhouse, used for school, Sunday school, and church. As far as the eye could reach, it was virgin prairie.

There was very little rain for two years after we came. All provisions, grain, and lumber were shipped on boats to Rulo. There was only an Indian trail between Rulo and Falls City. Everything was hauled over that trail.

After the drouth came the grasshoppers, and for two years they took all we had. The cattle barely lived grazing in the Nemaha valley. All grain was shipped in from Missouri.

The people had no amusements in the winter. In the summer they had picnics and a Methodist camp-meeting, on the Muddy river north of Falls City.

Over the Nemaha river two and one-half miles southwest of Falls City, on a high hill above the falls from which the town was named, was an Indian village. The Sac and Foxes and Iowa Indians occupied the village. Each spring and fall they went visiting other tribes, or other tribes visited them. They would march through the one street of Falls City with their ponies in single file. The tipi poles were strapped on each side of the ponies and their belongings and presents, for the tribe they were going to visit, piled on the poles. The men, women, and children walked beside the ponies, and the dogs brought up the rear. Sometimes, when the Indians had visitors, they would have a war-dance at night and the white people would go out to view it. Their bright fires, their scouts bringing in the news of hostile Indians in sight, and the hurried preparations to meet them, were quite exciting. The Indians were great beggars, and not very honest. We had to keep things under lock and key. They would walk right into the houses and say "Eat!" The women were all afraid of them and would give them provisions. If there was any food left after they had finished their eating, they would take it away with them.

Their burying-ground was very near the village. They buried their dead with all accoutrements, in a sitting posture in a grave about five feet deep, without covering.

177

The Indians cultivated small patches of land and raised corn, beans, pumpkins, etc. A man named Fisher now owns the land on which the Indians lived when I reached the country.

The people were very sociable. It was a healthy country, and we had health if very little else. We were young and the hardships did not seem so great as they do in looking backward fifty years.

NOTE—*Thyrza Reavis Roy was born August 7, 1834, in Cass county, Illinois, the daughter of Isham Reavis and Mahala Beck Reavis. Her great-grandfather, Isham Reavis, fought in the war of the Revolution. Her grandfather, Charles Reavis, and her own father, Isham Reavis, fought in the war of 1812. She is a real daughter of the war of 1812. She is a member of the U. S. Daughters of 1812, a member of the Deborah Avery Chapter D. A. R. of Lincoln, and a member of the Territorial Pioneers Association of Nebraska. Her husband, George Roy, died at Falls City March 2, 1903.*[19]

SEWARD COUNTY REMINISCENCES

COMPILED BY MARGARET HOLMES CHAPTER D. A. R.

Seward county shared with other counties all of the privations and experiences of pioneer life, though it seems to have had less trouble with hostile Indians than many localities in the state.

The struggles of pioneer settlers in the same country must necessarily be similar, though of course differing in detail. The first settlers deemed it important to locate on a stream where firewood could be obtained, and they were subject to high waters, prairie fires, constant fear of the Indian, and lack of provisions.

At one time the little band of settlers near the present site of Seward was reduced to one pan of corn, though they were not quite as reduced as their historic Pilgrim forefathers, when a load of provisions arrived that had been storm-bound.

Reminiscences are best at first hand, and the following letters, taken from the *History of Seward County* by W. W. Cox, recount some of the incidents of early pioneer life by those who really lived it.

Mrs. Sarah F. Anderson writes as follows:

"At the time of the great Indian scare of 1864, my father's family was one of the families which the Nebraska City people had heard were killed. It had been rumored throughout the little settlement that there were bands of hostile Indians approaching, and that they were committing great depredations as they went.

"One Sunday morning my uncle and Thomas Shields started down the river on a scouting expedition. After an all-day search, just at nightfall, they came suddenly upon an Indian camp. The men thought their time had come, but the redskins were equally scared. There was no chance to back out, and they resolved to know whether the Indians were friendly or hostile. As they bravely approached the camp, the Indians began to halloo, 'Heap good Omaha!' The men then concluded to camp over night with them, and they partook of a real Indian supper. The next morning, they went home satisfied that there were no hostile Indians in the country.

"A day or two after this, my father (William Imlay) and his brothers were on upper Plum creek haying, when Grandfather Imlay became frightened and hastened to our house and said the Indians were coming upon the settlement. He then hurried home to protect his own family. About three o'clock in the afternoon we saw a band of them approaching. They were about where the B. & M. depot now stands. We were living about eighty rods above the present iron bridge. My mother, thinking to escape them, locked the cabin door, and took all the children across the creek to the spring where she kept the milk. To kill time, she commenced churning. Very soon, four Indians (great, big, ugly creatures) came riding up to the spring and told mother that she was wanted over to the house. She said, 'No, I can't go; I am at work.' But they insisted in such a menacing manner that she felt obliged to yield and go. They said, 'Come, come,' in a most determined manner. The children all clinging to her, she started, and those great sneaking braves guarded her by one riding on each side, one before, and one behind. Poor mother and we four children had a slim show to escape. They watched our every movement, step by step.

180

When we reached the cabin, there sat sixteen burly Indians in a circle around the door. When we came up, they all arose and saluted mother, then sat down again. They had a young Indian interpreter. As they thought they had the family all thoroughly frightened, the young Indian began in good shape to tell just what they wanted. They would like to have two cows, two sacks of flour, and some meat. Mother saw that she must guard the provisions with desperation, as they had cost such great effort, having been hauled from the Missouri river. The Indians said, 'The Sioux are coming and will take all away, and we want some.' 'No,' said mother, 'we will take our cattle and provisions and go to Plattsmouth.' 'But,' said the Indian, 'they will be here tonight, and you can't get away.' Mother at this point began to be as much angry as frightened. 'I will not give you anything. You are lying to me. If the Sioux were so close, you would all be running yourselves.' At this point another brave, who had been pacing the yard, seeing mother grow so warm, picked up our axe and marched straight up to her and threw it down at her feet. She picked it up and stood it beside her. Mother said afterward that her every hair stood on end, but knowing that Indians respect bravery, she resolved to show no cowardice. We could all see that the whole river bend was swarming with Indians. Mother said with emphasis, 'I now want you to take your Indians and be gone at once.' Then they said, 'You are a brave squaw,' and the old chief motioned to his braves and they marched off to camp. The next day our family all went over to Plum creek and remained until things became settled.

"The following winter father was at Omaha attending the legislature; and I am sure that over a thousand Indians passed our place during the winter. It required pluck to withstand the thievish beggars. Sometimes they would sneak up and peep in at the window. Then others would beg for hours to get into the house.

"A great amount of snow had fallen, and shortly after father's return home, a heavy winter rain inundated all the bottom lands. We all came pretty near being drowned but succeeded in crawling out of the cabin at the rear window at midnight. Our only refuge

181

was a haystack, where we remained several days entirely surrounded by water, with no possible means of escape. Mr. Cox made several attempts to rescue us. First, he tried to cross the river in a molasses pan, and narrowly escaped being drowned, as the wind was high, and the stream filled with floating ice. The next day he made a raft and tried to cross, but the current was so rapid he could not manage it. It drifted against a tree where the water was ten feet deep, and the jar threw him off his balance, and the upper edge of the raft sank, so that the rapid current caught the raft and turned it on edge against the tree. Mr. Cox caught hold of a limb of the tree and saved himself from drowning. A desperate struggle ensued but he finally kicked and stamped until he got the raft on top of the water again, but it was wrong side up. We then gave up all hopes of getting help until the water subsided. The fourth day, tall trees were chopped by father on one side and by Mr. Cox on the other, and their branches interlocked, and we made our escape to his friendly cabin, where we found a kindly greeting, rest, food, and fire."

The following from the pen of Addison E. Sheldon is recorded in the same *History of Seward County*:

"My recollections of early Seward county life do not go back as far as the author's. They begin with one wind-blown day in September, 1869, when I, a small urchin from Minnesota, crossed the Seward county line near Pleasant Dale on my way with my mother and step-father (R. J. McCall), to the new home on the southeast quarter of section 18, town 9, range 2 east—about three miles southeast of the present Beaver Crossing. Looked back upon now, through all the intervening years, it seems to me there never was an autumn more supremely joyous, a prairie more entrancing, a woodland belt more alluring, a life more captivating than that which welcomed the new boy to the frontier in the beautiful West Blue valley. The upland 'divides' as I remember them were entirely destitute of settlement, and even along the streams, stretches of two, three, and five miles lay between nearest neighbors.

"What has become of the Nebraska wind of those days? I have sought it since far and wide in the Sand Hills and on the table lands of western Nebraska—that wind which blew ceaselessly, month after month, never pausing but to pucker its lips for a stronger blast! Where are the seas of rosin-weed, with their yellow summer parasols, which covered the prairie in those days? I have sought them too, and along gravelly ridges or some old ditch yet found a few degenerate descendants of the old-time host.

"Mention of merely a few incidents seeming to hold the drama and poetry of frontier life at that time: 'Pittsburgh, the city of vision, at the junction of Walnut creek and the West Blue, inhabited by a population of 20,000 people, with a glass factory, a paper factory, a brick factory, oil wells, a peat factory, woolen mills, junction of three railway lines, metropolis of the Blue Valley.' All this and so much more that I dare not attempt to picture it; a real existence in the brain of Christopher Lezenby in the years of 1871-72. What unwritten dramas sleep almost forgotten in the memories of early settlers! When Mr. Lezenby began to build his metropolis with the assistance of Attorney Boyd of Lincoln and a few other disinterested speculators, he was the possessor of several hundred acres of land, some hundreds of cattle, and other hundreds of hogs, and a fair, unmarried daughter. What pathetic memories of the old man, month after month, surveying off his beautiful farm into city lots for the new metropolis, while his cattle disappeared from the prairies and his swine from the oak thickets along the Walnut; with sublime and childish simplicity repeating day after day the confession of his faith that 'next week' work would begin; 'next week' the foundation for the factories would be laid; 'next week' the railway surveyors would set the grade stakes. And this real rural tragedy lasted through several years, ending in the loss of all his property, the marriage of his daughter to Irwin Stall, and the wandering forth of the old man until he died of a broken heart in California.

"One monument yet remains to mark the site and perpetuate the memory of Pittsburgh, a flowing well, found I think at the depth of twenty-eight feet in the year 1874 and continuously flowing since that. Strange that no one was wise enough to take the hint and that it was twenty years later before the second flowing well was struck at Beaver Crossing, leading to the systematic search for them which dotted the entire valley with their fountains.

"There were no high water bridges across the West Blue in those days. I remember acting as mail carrier for a number of families on the south bank of the Blue during the high waters of two or three summers, bringing the mail from the city of Pittsburgh post office on the north bank. A torn shirt and a pair of short-legged blue overalls—my entire wardrobe of those days—were twisted into a turban about my head, and plunging into the raging flood of the Blue which covered all the lower bottoms, five minutes' vigorous swimming carried me through the froth and foam and driftwood to the other side where I once more resumed my society clothes and, after securing the mail, upon my return to the river bank, tied it tightly in the turban and crossed the river as before.

"I remember my first lessons in political economy, the fierce fight between the northern and the southern parts of the county upon the question of voting bonds to the Midland Pacific railway during the years 1871-72. It was a sectional fight in fact, but in theory and in debate it was a contest over some first principles of government. The question of the people versus the corporation, since grown to such great proportions, was then first discussed to my childish ears. One incident of that contest is forever photographed on my brain—a crowd of one hundred farmers and villagers lounging in the shadow of T. H. Tisdale's old store. A yellow-skinned, emaciated lawyer from Lincoln who looked, to my boyish vision, like a Chinese chieftain from Manchuria, was speaking with fluent imaginative words in favor of the benefits the people of Seward county might secure by voting the bonds. This was H. W. Sommerlad, registrar of Lincoln land office. A short Saxon opponent, Rev. W. G. Keen of Walnut creek, was picked from the crowd by acclamation to reply to the Lincoln lawyer. The impression of his fiery words denouncing the aggressions of capital and appealing to the memories of the civil war and the

184

Revolutionary fathers to arouse the people's independence is with me yet.

"Next in the economic vista is the old Brisbin sod schoolhouse east of Walnut creek where a grange was organized. Here a lyceum was held through several winters in which the debates were strongly tinctured with the rising anti-monopoly sentiment of those hard times. George Michael and Charley Hunter, leaders of the boyish dare-deviltry of those days, were chosen as judges upon the debates in order to insure their good behavior, and they gravely decided for the negative or affirmative many deep discussions of doubtful themes.

"Beaver Crossing in the early days was remarkable for the great number of boys in its surrounding population, and I have observed in these later years when visiting there, that the custom of having boy babies in the family does not appear to have entirely gone out of fashion. That great swarm of restless boy population which gathered, sometimes two hundred strong, Saturday afternoons on the Common! What 'sleights of art and feats of strength' went round! What struggles of natural selection to secure a place upon the 'First Nine' of the baseball team! For years Beaver Crossing had the best baseball club in three or four counties, and some of her players won high laurels on distant diamonds.

"One custom which obtained in those frontier days seems to have been peculiar to the time, for I have not found it since in other frontier communities. It was the custom of 'calling off' the mail upon its arrival at the postoffice. The postmaster, old Tom Tisdale—a genuine facsimile of Petroleum V. Nasby—would dump the sacks of mail, brought overland on a buckboard, into a capacious box upon the counter of his store, then pick up piece by piece, and read the inscriptions thereon in a sonorous voice to the crowd, sometimes consisting of one or two hundred people. Each claimant would cry out 'Here!' when his name was called. Sometimes two-thirds of the mail was distributed in this way, saving a large amount of manual labor in pigeon-holing the same. Nasby had a happy and caustic freedom in commenting upon the mail during the performance, not always contemplated, I believe, by the United States postal regulations. A woman's handwriting upon a letter addressed to a young man was almost certain to receive some public notice from his sharp tongue, to the great enjoyment of the crowd and sometimes the visible annoyance of the young man. At one time he deliberately turned over a postal card written by a well-known young woman of Beaver Crossing who was away at school, and on observing that the message was written both horizontally and across, commented, 'From the holy mother, in Dutch.' If I should ever meet on the mystic other shore, which poets and philosophers have tried to picture for us, old Tom Tisdale, I would expect to see him with his spectacles pushed back from his nose, 'calling off' the mail to the assembled spirits, the while entertaining them with pungent personal epigrams.

"One startling picture arises from the past, framed as Browning writes 'in a sheet of flame'—the picture of the great prairie fire of October, 1871, which swept Seward county from south to north, leaving hardly a quarter section of continuous unburnt sod. A heavy wind, increasing to a hurricane, drove this fire down the West Blue valley. It jumped the Blue river in a dozen places as easily as a jack rabbit jumps a road. It left a great broad trail of cindered haystacks and smoking stables and houses. A neighbor of ours who was burnt out remarked that he had 'been through hell in one night,' and had 'no fear of the devil hereafter.'

"At the other end of the scale of temperature are recollections of the 'Great Storm' of April 13, 14, 15, 1873. There burst from a June atmosphere the worst blizzard in the history of the state. For three days it blew thick, freezing sleet, changing to snow so close and dense and dark that a man in a wagon vainly looked for the horses hitched to it through the storm. Men who were away from home lost their lives over the state. Stock was frozen to death. In sod houses, dugouts, and log cabins settlers huddled close about the hearth, burning enormous baskets of ten-cent corn to keep from freezing.

186

"In these later years of life, Fate has called me to make minute study of many historical periods and places. Yet my heart always turns to review the early scenes of settlement and civilization in Seward county with a peculiar thrill of personal emotion and special joy in the risen and rising fortunes of those who there built the foundations of a great commonwealth. No land can be dearer than the land of one's childhood and none can ever draw my thoughts further over plain or ocean than the happy valley upon West Blue whose waters spring spontaneously from beneath the soil to water her fortunate acres."

PIONEERING

BY GRANT LEE SHUMWAY

On September 15, 1885, I crossed the Missouri river at Omaha, and came west through Lincoln. The state fair was in full blast, but our party did not stop, as we were bound for Benkleman, Parks, and Haigler, Nebraska.

After looking over Dundy county, Nebraska, and Cheyenne county, Kansas, the rest of the party returned to Illinois.

I went to Indianola, and with Mr. Palmatier, I started for the Medicine. He carried the mail to Stockville and Medicine, which were newly established post offices in the interior to the north, and his conveyance was the hind wheels of an ordinary wagon, to which he had fashioned a pair of thills. He said that he was using such a vehicle because it enabled him to cut off several miles in the very rough country through which we passed.

The jolting was something fierce but being young and used to riding in lumber wagons, I did not mind. I was very much interested in everything, but the things that linger most clearly in my mind after all these years are the bushy whiskered, hopeful faces of the men who greeted us from dugouts and sod cabins. The men's eyes were alight with enthusiasm and candor, but I do not remember of having seen a woman or child upon the trip.

It seems that men can drop back into the primitive so much more easily than women: not perhaps with all the brutality of the First Men, but they can adjust themselves to the environment of the wilderness, and the rusticity of the frontier, with comparative ease.

I stopped for the night in Hay cañon, a branch of Lake cañon, at Hawkins brothers' hay camp, and I remember when they told me that they had three hundred tons of hay in the stack, that it seemed almost an inconceivable quantity. On our old Illinois farm twenty-five or thirty tons seemed a large amount, but three hundred tons was beyond our range of reasoning. However, we now stack that much on eighty acres in the Scottsbluff country.

In due time I went on over the great tableland to the city of North Platte, and going down the cañon on the south side of the south river, I killed my first jack rabbit, an event which seemed to make me feel more of a westerner than any circumstance up to that time.

My first impression of North Platte, with its twelve saloons, was not of the best. And my conception of Buffalo Bill dropped several notches in esteem when I saw the Wild West saloon. But in the light of years, I am less puritanical in my views of the first people of the plains. In subsequent years I rode the range as a cowboy, and drove twenty-mule teams with a single line and a black-snake, and while always I remained an abstainer and occasionally found others that did likewise, I learned to tolerate, and then enjoy, the witticisms and foolishness of those that did indulge. Sometimes the boys in their cups would "smoke up" the little cities of the plains, but they never felt any resentment if one of their number did not participate in their drinking and festive sports.

I spent the winter of 1885 on the ranch of Hall & Evans, near North Platte, and one of the pleasantest acquaintanceships of my life has been that of John Evans, now registrar of the land office at North Platte.

In the spring of '86 the constant stream of emigrant wagons going west gave one an impression that in a little time the entire West would be filled, and I grew impatient to be upon my way and secure selections. In May I arrived at Sidney and from there rode in a box car to Cheyenne. When we topped the divide east of Cheyenne, I saw the snow-capped peaks of the Rockies for the first time.

During the summer I "skinned mules," aiding in the construction of the Cheyenne & Northern, now a part of the Hill system that connects Denver with the Big Horn basin and Puget sound.

Returning to Sidney in the autumn, I fell in with George Hendricks, who had been in the mines for twenty years and finally gave it up. We shoveled coal for the Union Pacific until we had a grub stake for the winter. I purchased a broncho, and upon him we packed our belongings—beds, blankets, tarpaulin, provisions, cooking utensils, tools, and clothing, and started north over the divide for "Pumpkin creek," our promised land. In a little over a day's travel, one leading the horse and the other walking behind to prod it along, we reached Hackberry cañon, and here, in a grove by a spring, we built our first cabin.

Three sides were log, the cracks filled with small pieces of wood and plastered with mud from the spring, and the back of the cabin was against a rock, and up this rock we improvised a fireplace, with loose stones and mud.

When we had rigged a bunk of native red cedar along the side of this rude shelter, and the fire was burning in our fireplace, the coffee steaming, the bread baking in the skillet, the odor of bacon frying, and the wind whistling through the tree-tops, that cabin seemed a mighty cozy place.

We could sometimes hear the coyotes and the grey wolves howl at night, but a sense of security prevailed, and our sleep was sound. Out of the elements at hand, we had made the rudiments of a home on land that was to become ours—our very own—forever.

Born at Oxford, Illinois, on March 7, 1865, Grant Lee Shumway came to Banner County (then Cheyenne County), Nebraska, in 1885, where he filed a homestead. He married Gertrude Viola Ashford, at Ashford, Nebraska, on September 10, 1890. He published The Ashford Advocate for several years before moving to Scottsbluff in 1901 where he started the Pathfinder Land Company. Shumway was a member of the Robert W. Furnas Lodge No. 265 A.F. & A.M. and a charter member of Hannibal Lodge No. 40, Scottsbluff Knights of Pythias.

In 1917 and 1918 Shumway served as State Commissioner of Public Lands and Buildings. He also served for a time as Secretary of Agriculture under Governor Charles Bryan. Shumway was an author and poet, as well as editor of The History of Western Nebraska and Its People, published in 1921. Grant Lee Shumway died on November 7, 1925, as a result of complications following gall stone surgery. He was laid to rest at the Fairview Cemetery at Scottsbluff.[20]

---

[20] https://history.nebraska.gov/collections/grant-lee-shumway-rg1381am

EARLY DAYS IN STANTON COUNTY

STATEMENT BY ANDREW J. BOTTORFF

I came to Nebraska at the close of the civil war, having served during the entire campaign with the Seventeenth Indiana regiment. I came west with oxen and wagon in the fall of 1866, bringing my family. We wintered at Rockport, but as soon as spring opened went to Stanton county, where I took a homestead. Here we had few neighbors and our share of hardships but thrived and were happy.

One day I heard my dogs barking and found them down in a ravine, near the Elkhorn river, with an elk at bay, and killed him with my axe.

The first year I was appointed county surveyor. Having no instruments at hand, I walked to Omaha, over a hundred miles distant, and led a fat cow to market there. I sold the cow but found no instruments. I was told of a man at Fort Calhoun who had an outfit I might get, so wended my way there. I found E. H. Clark, who would sell me the necessary supplies, and I bought them; then carried them, with some other home necessities obtained in Omaha, back to Stanton, as I had come, on foot.

I am now seventy-five years old, and have raised a large family; yet wife and I are as happy and spry as if we had never worked, and are enjoying life in sunny California, where we have lived for the last ten years.

Statement by Sven Johanson

With my wife and two small children I reached Omaha, Nebraska, June 26, 1868. We came direct from Norway, having crossed the stormy Atlantic in a small sailboat, the voyage taking eight weeks.

A brother who had settled in Stanton county, 107 miles from Omaha, had planned to meet us in that city. After being there a few days this brother, together with two other men, arrived and we were very happy. With two yoke of oxen and one team of horses, each hitched to a load of lumber, we journeyed from Omaha to Stanton county. Arriving there, we found shelter in a small dugout with our brother and family, where we remained until we filed on a homestead and had built a dugout of our own.

We had plenty of clothing, a good lot of linens and homespun materials, but these and ten dollars in money were all we possessed.

The land office was at Omaha and it was necessary for me to walk there to make a filing. I had to stop along the way wherever I could secure work, and in that way got some food, and occasionally earned a few cents, and this enabled me to purchase groceries to carry back to my family. There were no bridges across rivers or creeks, and we were compelled to swim; at one time in particular I was very thankful I was a good swimmer. A brother-in-law and myself had gone to Fremont, Nebraska, for employment, and on our return, we found the Elkhorn river almost out of its banks. This frightened my companion, who could not swim, but I told him to be calm, we would come to no harm. I took our few groceries and our clothing and swam across, then going back for my companion, who was a very large man, I took him on my back and swam safely to the other shore.

While I was away, my family would be holding down our claim and taking care of our one cow. We were surrounded by Indians, and there were no white people west of where we lived.

In the fall of 1869, we secured a yoke of oxen, and the following spring hauled home logs from along the river and creek and soon had a comfortable log house erected.

Thus we labored and saved little by little until we were able to erect a frame house, not hewn by hand, but made from real lumber, and by this time we felt well repaid for the many hardships we had endured. The old "homestead" is still our home, but the dear, faithful, loving mother who so bravely bore all the hardships of early days was called to her rich reward January 28, 1912. She was born June 15, 1844, and I was born October 14, 1837.

FRED E. ROPER, PIONEER

By Ernest E. Correll

Fred E. Roper, a pioneer of Hebron, Nebraska, was eighty years old on October 10, 1915. Sixty-one years ago, Mr. Roper "crossed the plains," going from New York state to California.

Eleven years more than a half-century—and to look back upon the then barren stretch of the country in comparison with the present fertile region of prosperous homes and populous cities, takes a vivid stretch of imagination to realize the dreamlike transformation. At that time San Francisco was a village of about five hundred persons living in adobe huts surrounded by a mud wall for a fortified protection from the marauding Indians.

Fred E. Roper was born in Candor Hill, New York, October 10, 1835. When three years old he moved with his parents to Canton, Bradford county, Pennsylvania, and later moved with his brother to Baraboo, Wisconsin. Then he shipped as a "hand" on a raft going down the Wisconsin and Mississippi rivers to St. Louis, getting one dollar a day and board. He returned north on a steamer, stopping at Burlington, Iowa, where his sister resided.

In 1854, when he was nineteen years of age, Mr. Roper "started west." His sister walked to the edge of the town with him as he led his one-horned cow, which was to furnish milk for coffee on the camp-out trip, which was to last three months, enroute to the Pacific coast.

There were three outfits—a horse train, mule train, and ox train. Mr. Roper traveled in an ox train of twenty-five teams. The travelers elected officers from among those who had made the trip before, and military discipline prevailed.

At nights, the men took turns at guard duty in relays—from dark to midnight and from midnight to dawn, when the herder was called to turn the cattle out to browse. One man herded them until breakfast was ready, and another man herded them until time to yoke up. This overland train was never molested by the Indians, although one night some spying Cheyennes were made prisoners under guard over night until the oxen were yoked up and ready to start.

The prospectors crossed the Missouri river at Omaha, which at that time had no residences or business buildings. Enroute to Salt Lake City, the South Platte route was followed, averaging about twenty miles a day. Enough provisions were carried to last through the journey and as they had some provisions left when they reached Salt Lake City, they were sold to the half-starved Mormons at big prices.

Some perplexing difficulties were encountered on the journey. At one point in the mountains, beyond Salt Lake City, the trail was so narrow that the oxen were unhitched and led single file around the cliff, while the wagons were taken apart and lowered down the precipice with ropes.

When crossing the desert, additional water had to be carried in extra kegs and canteens. When the tired cattle got near enough to the river to smell the fresh water, they pricked up their ears, stiffened their necks, and made a rush for the stream, so the men had to stand in front of them until the chains were loosened to prevent their crazily dashing into the water with the wagons.

Mr. Roper worked by the day for three months in the mines northeast of San Francisco. While placer mining, he one day picked up a gold nugget, from which his engagement ring was made by a jeweler in San Francisco, and worn by Mrs. Roper until her death, October 28, 1908. The ring was engraved with two hearts with the initials M. E. R. and is now in the possession of their son Maun, whose initials are the same.

Mr. Roper was one of a company of three men who worked a claim that had been once worked over, on a report that there was a crevasse that had not been bottomed. The first workers did not have "quicksilver," which is necessary to catch fine gold, but Mr. Roper's company had a jug shipped from San Francisco. Nothing less than a fifty-pound jug of quicksilver would be sold, at fifty cents a pound. This was used in sluice-boxes as "quicksilver riffles," to catch the fine float gold, when it would instantly sink to the bottom of the quicksilver, while the dirt and stones would wash over; the coarse rock would be first tossed out with a sluice-fork (similar to a flat-tined pitchfork). In three years the three men worked the mine out, making about fifteen hundred dollars apiece.

With his share carried in buckskin sacks belted around his waist under his clothes, Mr. Roper started in a sailing vessel up north along the coast on a trip, hunting for richer diggings. Then he went on a steamer to the Isthmus of Panama, which he crossed with a hired horse team, then by steamer to New York and by railroad to Philadelphia to get his gold minted.

After his marriage in 1861 Mr. Roper returned to the West and in '64 ran a hotel at Beatrice called "Pat's Cabin." When Nebraska voted on the question of admission to statehood, Mr. Roper's ballot was vote No. 3.

Desiring to get a home of his own, Fred Roper came on west into what is now Thayer county, and about six miles northwest of the present site of Hebron up the Little Blue, he bought out the preëmption rights of Bill and Walt Hackney, who had "squatted" there with the expectation of paying the government the customary $1.25 per acre. In certain localities those claims afterwards doubled to $2.50 per acre. Mr. Roper paid only the value of the log cabin and log stables, and came into possession of the eighty acres, which he homesteaded, and later bought adjoining land for $1.25 per acre.

Occasionally he made trips to St. Joe and Nebraska City for supplies, which he freighted overland to Hackney ranch. At that time Mr. Roper knew every man on the trail from the Missouri river to Kearney. On these trips he used to stop with Bill McCandles, who was shot with three other victims by "Wild Bill" on Rock creek in Jefferson county.

The first house at Hackney ranch was burned by the Cheyenne Indians in their great raid of 1864, at which time Miss Laura Roper (daughter of Joe B. Roper) and Mrs. Eubanks were captured by the Indians near Fox Ford in Nuckolls county and kept in captivity until ransomed by Colonel Wyncoop of the U. S. army for $1,000. Si Alexander of Meridian (southeast of the present town of Alexandria), was with the government troops at the time of Miss Roper's release near Denver. Her parents, believing her dead, had meanwhile moved back to New York state. (Laura Roper is still alive, being now Mrs. Laura Vance, at Skiatook, Oklahoma.) At the time of the above-mentioned raid, the Indians at Hackney ranch threw the charred cottonwood logs of the house into the well, to prevent travelers from getting water. Fred Roper was then at Beatrice, having just a few days before sold Hackney ranch to an overland traveler. After the raid, the new owner deserted the place, in the fall of 1869, and in a few months, Mr. Roper returned from Beatrice and again preempted the same place.

In 1876 Mr. and Mrs. Roper moved to Meridian and ran a tavern for about a year, then moved back to Hackney, where they resided until the fall of 1893, when they moved into Hebron to make their permanent home. Mr. Roper was postmaster at Hebron for four years under Cleveland's last administration.

An Indian Raid

By Ernest E. Correll

In 1869, Fayette Kingsley and family resided on the Haney homestead at the southeast corner of Hebron, where Mr. Haney had been brutally murdered in the presence of his three daughters in 1867, the daughters escaping and eventually reaching their home, "back east."

On May 26, 1869, "Old Daddy" Marks, accompanied by a young man for protection, drove over from Rose creek to warn Kingsley's that the Indians were on a raid. While they were talking, Mr. Kingsley heard the pit-pat of the Indian horses on the wet prairie. From the west were riding thirty-six Indians, led by a white man, whose hat and fine boots attracted attention in contrast to the bare-headed Indians wearing moccasins.

In the house were enough guns and revolvers to shoot sixty rounds without loading. When Mrs. Kingsley saw the Indians approaching, she scattered the arms and ammunition on the table where the men could get them. There were two Spencer carbines, a double-barreled shotgun, and two navy revolvers, besides other firearms.

Mr. Kingsley and Charlie Miller (a young man from the East who was boarding with them) went into the house, got the guns, and leveled them on the Indians, who had come within 250 yards of the log-house, but who veered off on seeing the guns. One of the party at the house exclaimed, "The Indians are going past and turning off!" Mr. Marks then said, "Then for God's sake, don't shoot!"

The Indians went on down the river and drove away eleven of King Fisher's horses. Two of Fisher's boys lay concealed in the grass and saw the white leader of the Indians remove his hat, showing his close-cut hair. He talked the Indian language and ordered the redskins to drive up a pony, which proved to be lame and was not taken. The Indians continued their raid nearly to Meridian.

Meanwhile at Kingsley's preparations were made for a hurried flight. Mr. Marks said he must go home to protect his own family on Rose creek, but the young man accompanying him insisted that he cross the river and return by way of Alexander's ranch on the Big Sandy, as otherwise they would be following the Indians. Mr. Kingsley, with his wife and three children, went with them to Alexander's ranch, staying there two weeks until Governor Butler formed a company of militia composed of the settlers, to protect the frontier. A company of the Second U. S. Cavalry was sent here and stationed west of Hackney, later that summer. The Indians killed a man and his son, and took their horses, less than two miles from the soldiers' camp.

On returning to the homestead, two cows and two yoke of oxen were found all right. Before the flight, Mr. Kingsley had torn down the pen, letting out a calf and a pig. Sixty days later, on recovering the pig, Mr. Kingsley noticed a sore spot on its back, and he pulled out an arrow point about three inches long.

The Indians had taken all the bedding and eatables, even taking fresh baked bread out of the oven. They tore open the feather-bed and scattered the contents about—whether for amusement or in search of hidden treasures is not known. They found a good pair of boots and cut out the fine leather tops (perhaps for moccasins) but left the heavy soles. From a new harness they also took all the fine straps and left the tugs and heavy leather. They had such a load that at the woodpile they discarded Mr. Kingsley's double-barreled shotgun, which had been loaded with buckshot for them.

Captain Wilson, a lawyer who boarded with Mr. Kingsley, had gone to warn King Fisher, leaving several greenbacks inside a copy of the Nebraska statutes. These the Indians found and appropriated—perhaps their white leader was a renegade lawyer accustomed to getting money out of the statutes.

In 1877 Mr. Kingsley's family had a narrow escape from death in a peculiar manner. After a heavy rain, the walls of his basement caved in. His children occupied two beds standing end to end and filling the end of the basement. When the rocks from the wall caved in, both beds were crushed to the floor and a little pet dog on one of the beds was killed, but the children had no bones broken. Presumably, the bedding protected them, and the breaking of the bedsteads broke the jar of the rocks on their bodies.

Mr. Kingsley has a deeply religious nature and believes that Divine protection has been with him through life.

REMINISCENCES

BY MRS. E. A. RUSSELL

In September, 1884, Rev. E. A. Russell was transferred by the American Baptist Publication Society from his work in the East to Nebraska, and settled on an eighty-acre ranch near Ord. Mr. Russell had held pastorates for twenty-six years in New Hampshire, New York, and Indiana, but desired to come west for improvement in health. He was accompanied by his family of seven. Western life was strange and exciting with always the possibility of an Indian raid, and dangerous prairie fires. It was the custom to plow a wide furrow around the home buildings as a precaution against the latter.

The first year in Nebraska, our oldest daughter, Alice M. Russell, was principal of the Ord school, and Edith taught in the primary grade.

On the fifth of August 1885, late in the afternoon, a terrific hail-storm swept over the country. All crops were destroyed; even the grass was beaten into the earth, so there was little left as pasture for cattle. Pigs and poultry were killed by dozens and the plea of a tender-hearted girl, that a poor calf, beaten down by hailstones, might be brought "right into the kitchen," was long remembered. Not a window in our house remained unbroken. The floor was covered with rain and broken glass and ice; and our new, white, hard-finished walls and ceilings were bespattered and disfigured.

This hail-storm was a general calamity. The whole country suffered, and many families returned, disheartened, to friends in the East.

The Baptist church was so shattered that, for its few members, it was no easy task to repair it. But they soon put it in good condition, only to see it utterly wrecked by a small cyclone the following October.

The income that year from a forty-acre cornfield was one small "nubbin" less than three inches in length.

All these things served to emphasize the heart-rending stories we had heard of sufferings of early pioneers. The nervous shock sustained by the writer was so great that a year elapsed before she was able to see clearly, or to read. As she was engaged on the four years' post-graduate course of the Chautauqua Literary and Scientific Circle, her eldest son read aloud to her during that year and her work was completed at the same time as he and his younger sister graduated with the class of 1887.

Some time later the writer organized a Chautauqua Circle, Ord's first literary society. Its president was a Mr. King and its secretary E. J. Clements, now of Lincoln, Nebraska.

During our second winter in Nebraska the writer did not see a woman to speak to after her daughters went to their schools in Lincoln, where one was teaching and the other a University pupil.

Of the "Minnie Freeman Storm" in January 1888, all our readers have doubtless heard. Our two youngest boys were at school a mile away; but fortunately, we lived south of town and they reached home in safety.

In 1881 Fort Hartsuff, twelve miles away, had been abandoned. The building of this fort had been the salvation of pioneers, giving them work and wages after the terrible scourge of locusts in 1874.

It was still the pride of those who had been enabled to remain in the desolated country and we heard much about it. So, when a brother came from New England to visit an only sister on the "Great American Desert," we took an early start one morning and visited "The Fort." The buildings, at that time, were in fairly good condition. Officers' quarters, barracks, commissary buildings, stables, and other structures were of concrete, so arranged as to form a hollow square; and, near by on a hill, was a circular stockade, which was said to be connected with the fort by an underground passage.

A prominent figure in Ord in 1884 was an attractive young lady who later married Dr. F. D. Haldeman. In 1904 Mrs. Haldeman organized *Coronado* chapter, Daughters of the American Revolution. Her sister, Dr. Minerva Newbecker, has practiced medicine in Ord for many years. Another sister, Clara Newbecker, has long been a teacher in the public schools of Chicago. These three sisters, who descended from Lieutenant Philip Newbecker, of Revolutionary fame, and Mrs. Nellie Coombs, are the only living charter members of *Coronado* chapter. The chapter was named in honor of that governor of New Galicia in Mexico who is supposed to have passed through some portion of our territory in 1540 when he fitted out an expedition to seek and Christianize the people of that wonderful region where "golden bells and dishes of solid gold" hung thick upon the trees.

About all that is definitely known is that he set up a cross at the big river, with the inscription: "Thus far came Francisco de Coronado, General of an expedition."

And now, in 1915, the family of seven, by one marriage after another, has dwindled to a lonely—two.

The head of our household, with recovered health, served his denomination twenty years in this great field, comprising Nebraska, Upper Colorado, and Wyoming. He retired in 1904 to the sanctuary of a quiet home.

REMINISCENCES OF FORT CALHOUN

BY W. H. ALLEN

I reached Fort Calhoun in May 1856, with my friends, Mr. and
Mrs. John Allen, coming with team and wagon from Edgar county,
Illinois. I was then eleven years old. Fort Calhoun had no soldiers,
but some of the Fort Atkinson buildings were still standing. I
remember the liberty pole, the magazine, the old brick-yard, at
which places we children played and picked up trinkets. There was
one general store then, kept by Pink Allen and Jascoby, and but
few settlers. Among those I remember were, my uncle, Thomas
Allen; E. H. Clark, a land agent; Col. Geo. Stevens and family,
who started a hotel in 1856, and Orrin Rhoades, whose family
lived on a claim five miles west of town. That summer my father
took a claim near Rhoades', building a log house and barn at the
edge of the woods. We moved there in the fall and laid in a good
supply of wood for the huge fireplace, used for cooking as well as
heating. Our rations were scanty, consisting of wild game for meat,
corn bread, potatoes and beans purchased at Fort Calhoun. The
next spring, we cleared some small patches for garden and corn,
which we planted and tended with a hoe. There were no houses
between ours and Fort Calhoun, nor any bridges. Rhoades' house
and ours were the only ones between Fontenelle and Fort Calhoun.
Members of the Quincy colony at Fontenelle went to Council

Bluffs for flour and used our place as a half-way house, stopping each way over night. How we children did enjoy their company, and stories of the Indians. We were never molested by the red men, only that they would come begging food occasionally.

I had no schooling until 1860 when I worked for my board in Fort Calhoun at E. H. Clark's and attended public school a few months. The next two years I did likewise, boarding at Alex. Reed's.

From 1866 to 1869 inclusive I cut cord-wood and railroad ties which I hauled to Omaha for use in the building of the Union Pacific railroad. I received from $8.00 to $15.00 per cord for my wood, and $1.00 each for ties.

Deer were plentiful and once when returning from Omaha I saw an old deer and fawn. Unhitching my team, I jumped on one horse and chased the young one down, caught and tamed it. I put a bell on its neck and let it run about at will. It came to its sleeping place every night until the next spring when it left, never to be seen by us again.

In the fall of 1864, I was engaged by Edward Creighton to freight with a wagon train to Denver, carrying flour and telegraph supplies. The cattle were corralled and broke at Cole's creek, west of Omaha known then as "Robber's Roost," and I thought it great fun to yoke and break those wild cattle. We started in October with forty wagons, seven yoke of oxen to each wagon. I went as far as Fort Cottonwood, one hundred miles beyond Fort Kearny, reaching there about November 20. There about a dozen of us grew tired of the trip and turned back with a wagon and one ox team. On our return, at Plum creek, thirty-five miles west of Fort Kearny we saw where a train had been attacked by Indians, oxen killed, wagons robbed and abandoned. We waded the rivers, Loup Fork and Platte, which was a cold bath at that time of year.

I lived at this same place in the woods until I took a homestead three miles farther west in 1868.

My father's home was famous at that time, also years afterward, as a beautiful spot, in which to hold Fourth of July celebrations, school picnics, etc., and the hospitality and good cooking of my mother, "Aunt Polly Allen" as she was familiarly called, was known to all the early settlers in this section of the country.

REMINISCENCES OF WASHINGTON COUNTY

BY MRS. EMILY BOTTORFF ALLEN

I came to Washington county, Nebraska, with my parents in the fall of 1865, by ox team from Indiana. We stopped at Rockport, where father and brothers got work at wood chopping. They built a house by digging into a hill and using logs to finish the front. The weather was delightful, and autumn's golden tints in the foliage were beautiful.

We gathered hazel nuts and wild grapes, often scaring a deer from the underbrush. Our neighbors were the Shipleys, who were very hospitable, and shared their garden products with us.

During the winter father bought John Frazier's homestead, but our home was still in a dugout, in which we were comfortable. We obtained all needed supplies from Fort Calhoun or Omaha.

In the spring Amasa Warrick, from Cuming City, came to our home in search of a teacher and offered me the position, which I accepted. Elam Clark of Fort Calhoun endorsed my teacher's certificate. I soon commenced teaching at Cuming City, and pupils came for miles around. I boarded at George A. Brigham's. Mr.

Brigham was county surveyor, postmaster, music teacher, as well as land agent, and a very fine man.

One day, while busy with my classes, the door opened and three large Indians stole in, seating themselves near the stove. I was greatly alarmed and whispered to one of my pupils to hasten to the nearest neighbor for assistance. As soon as the lad left, one Indian went to the window and asked, "Where boy go?" I said, "I don't know." The three Indians chattered together a moment, and then the spokesman said. "I kill you sure," but seeing a man coming in the distance with a gun, they all hurried out and ran over the hill.

I taught at Cuming City until the school fund was exhausted, and by that time the small schoolhouse on Long creek was completed. Allen Craig and Thomas McDonald were directors. I boarded at home and taught the first school in this district, with fourteen pupils enrolled. At this time Judge Bowen of Omaha was county superintendent, and I went there to have my certificate renewed.

When all the public money in the Long Creek district was used up, I went back to Cuming City to teach. The population of this district had increased to such an extent that I needed an assistant, and I was authorized to appoint one of my best pupils to the position. I selected Vienna Cooper, daughter of Dr. P. J. Cooper. I boarded at the Lippincott home, known as the "Halfway House" on the stage line between Omaha and Decatur. It was a stage station where horses were changed, and drivers and passengers stopped over night.

At the close of our summer term we held a picnic and entertainment on the Methodist church grounds, using the lumber for the new church for our platform and seats. This entertainment was pronounced the grandest affair ever held in the West.

The school funds of the Cuming City district being again exhausted, I returned to Long Creek district in the fall of 1867, and taught as long as there was any money in the treasury. By that time, the village of Blair had sprung up, absorbing Cuming City and De Soto, and I was employed to teach in their new log schoolhouse. T. M. Carter was director of the Blair district. Orrin Colby of Bell Creek was county superintendent, and he visited the schools of the county, making the rounds on foot. I taught at Blair until April 1869, when I was married to William Henry Allen, a pioneer of Fort Calhoun. Our license was issued by Judge Stilts of Fort Calhoun, where we were married by Dr. Andrews. We raised our family in the Long Creek district, and still reside where we settled in those pioneer days.

Emily Allen is the daughter of Andrew Jackson Bottorff, from page 259.

Ruth Emily Bottorff Allen[21]

---

[21] https://www.findagrave.com/memorial/37655063/ruth-emily-allen

REMINISCENCES OF DE SOTO IN 1855

BY OLIVER BOUVIER

Mother Bouvier, a kind old soul, who settled in De Soto in the summer of 1855, had many hardships. Just above her log house, on the ridge, was the regular Indian trail and the Indians made it a point to stop at our house regularly, as they went to Fort Calhoun or to Omaha. She befriended them many times and they always treated her kindly. "Omaha Mary," who was often a caller at our house was always at the head of her band. She was educated and could talk French well to us.

What she said was law with all the Indians. Our creek was thick with beavers and as a small boy I could not trap them, but she could, and had her traps there and collected many skins from our place. I wanted her to show me the trick of it, but she would never allow me to follow her. At one time I sneaked along, and she caught me in the act and grabbed me by the collar and with a switch in her hand, gave me a severe warning.

This same squaw was an expert with bow and arrow, and I have seen her speedily cross the Missouri river in a canoe with but one oar. Our wall was always black and greasy by the Indians sitting against it while they ate the plates of mush and sorghum my mother served them. I have caught many buffalo calves out on the prairies, and one I brought to our De Soto home and tamed it. My sister Adeline and myself tried to break it to drive with an ox hitched to a sled, but never succeeded to any great extent. One day Joseph La Flesche came along and offered us $50.00 for it and we sold it to him but he found he could not separate it from our herd, so bought a heifer, which it would follow and Mr. Joseph Boucha and myself took them up to the reservation for him. He entertained us warmly at his Indian quarters for two or three days. I have cured many buffalo steak (by the Indian method) and we used the meat on our table.

Oliver Bouvier was the son of Louis and Eugenia (Courvoisier) Bouvier. The family settled in DeSoto, Nebraska in 1856. Oliver enlisted on October 17, 1862 and served in the Co. B, 2nd Regiment. He married Coralena Hoylan on October 19, 1881. They were the parents of Esther and Ina.[22]

[22] https://www.findagrave.com/memorial/57412095/oliver-bouvier

THE STORY OF THE TOWN OF FONTENELLE

BY MRS. EDA MEAD

When Nebraska was first organized as a territory, a party of people in Quincy, Illinois, conceived the idea of starting a city in the new territory and thus making their fortune. They accordingly sent out a party of men to select a site.

These men reached Omaha in 1854. There they met Logan Fontenelle, chief of the Omahas, who held the land along the Platte and Elkhorn rivers. He agreed to direct them to a place favorable for a town. Upon reaching the spot, where the present village is now situated, they were so pleased that they did not look farther but paid the chief one hundred dollars for the right to claim and locate twenty square miles of land. This consisted of land adjoining the Elkhorn river, then ascending a high bluff, a tableland ideal for the location of the town.

These men thought the Elkhorn was navigable and that they could ship their goods from Quincy by way of the Missouri, Platte, and Elkhorn rivers.

Early in the spring of 1855 a number of the colonists, bringing their household goods, left Quincy on a small boat, the "Mary Cole," expecting to reach Fontenelle by way of the Elkhorn; and then use the boat as a packet to points on the Platte and Elkhorn rivers.

But the boat struck a snag in the Missouri and, with a part of the cargo, was lost. The colonists then took what was saved overland to Fontenelle.

By the first of May 1855, there were sufficient colonists on the site to hold the claims. Then each of the fifty members drew by lot for the eighteen lots each one was to hold. The first choice fell to W. H. Davis. He chose the land along the river, fully convinced of its superior situation as a steamboat landing.

The colonists then built houses of cottonwood timber, and a store and hotel were started. Thus, the little town of about two hundred inhabitants was started with great hopes of soon becoming a large city.

Land on the edge of the bluff had been set aside for a college building. This was called Collegeview. Here a building was begun in 1856 and completed in 1859. This was the first advanced educational institution to be chartered west of the Missouri river.

In 1865 this building was burned. Another building was immediately erected, but after a few years' struggle for patronage, they found it was doomed to die, so negotiated with the people of Crete, Nebraska, and the Congregational organizations (for it was built by the Congregationalists) in Nebraska. It therefore became the nucleus of what is now Doane College.

The bell of the old building is still in use in the little village.

The first religious services were held by the Congregationalists. The church was first organized by Rev. Reuben Gaylord, who also organized the First Congregational church in Omaha.

In Fontenelle the Congregationalists did not have a building but worshiped in the college. This church has long since ceased to exist, but strange as it may seem after so many years, the last regular pastor was the same man, Rev. Reuben Gaylord, who organized it.

There was a little band of fifteen Methodists; this was called the Fontenelle Mission. In 1857 an evangelist, Jerome Spillman, was sent to take charge of this little mission. He soon had a membership of about three score people. A church was organized, and a building and parsonage completed. This prospered with the town, but as the village began to lose ground the church was doomed to die. The building stood vacant for a number of years but was finally moved to Arlington.

The settlers found the first winter of 1855-56 mild and agreeable. They thought that this was a sample of the regular winter climate; so, when the cold, blizzardy, deep-snow winter of 1856-57 came it found the majority ill prepared. Many were living in log cabins which had been built only for temporary use. The roofs were full of holes and just the dirt for floors.

On awaking in the morning after the first blizzard many found their homes drifted full of snow; even the beds were covered. The snow lay four or five feet deep on the level and the temperature was far below zero.

Most of the settlers lost all of their stock. Food was scarce, but wild game was plentiful. Mr. Sam Francis would take his horse and gun and hunt along the river. The settlers say he might be seen many times that winter coming into the village with two deer tied to his horse's tail trailing in the snow. By this means, he saved many of the colonists from starvation.

Provisions were very high priced. Potatoes brought four and five dollars a bushel; bacon and pork could not be had at any price. One settler is said to have sold a small hog for forty-five dollars; with this he bought eighty acres of land, which is today worth almost one hundred eighty dollars an acre.

A sack of flour cost from ten to fifteen dollars.

At this time many who had come just for speculation left, thus only the homebuilders or those who had spent their all and could not return, remained.

Then came trouble with the Indians. In the year 1859 the Pawnees were not paid by the government, for some reason. They became desperate and began stealing cattle from the settlers along the Elkhorn around Fontenelle. The settlers of Fontenelle formed a company known as the "Fontenelle Mounted Rangers," and together with a company sent out by Governor Black from Omaha with one piece of light artillery, started after the Pawnees who were traveling west and north.

They captured six prisoners and held them bound. While they were camped for rest, a squaw in some way gave a knife to one of the prisoners. He pretended to kill himself by cutting his breast and mouth so that he bled freely. He then dropped as if dead. Amidst the confusion the other five, whose ropes had been cut, supposedly by this same squaw, escaped.

As the settlers were breaking camp to still pursue the fleeing tribe, they wondered what to do with the dead Indian. Someone expressed doubt as to his really being dead. Then one of the settlers raised his gun and said he would soon make sure. No sooner had the gun been aimed than the Indian jumped to his feet and said, "Whoof! Me no sick!" They then journeyed on to attack the main tribe. When near their camp the settlers formed a semi-circle on a hill, with the artillery in the center.

As soon as the Indians saw the settlers, they came riding as swiftly as possible to make an attack, but when within a short distance and before the leader of the settlers could call "Fire!" they retreated. They advanced and retreated in this way three times. The settlers were at a loss to understand just what the Indians intended to do; but decided that they did not know of the artillery until near enough to see it, then were afraid to make the attack, so tried to scare the settlers, but failing to do this they finally advanced with a white rag tied to a stick.

The Indians agreed to be peaceable and stop the thieving if the settlers would pay for a pony which had been accidentally killed and give them medicine for the sick and wounded.

Some of the men who took part in this fight say that if the leader had ordered the settlers to fire on the first advance of the Indians every settler would have been killed. There were twice as many Indians in the first place and the settlers afterwards found that not more than one-third of their guns would work; and after they had fired once, while they were reloading, the Indians with their bows and arrows would have exterminated them. They consider it was the one piece of light artillery that saved them, as the Indians were very much afraid of a cannon. This ended any serious Indian trouble, but the housewives had to be ever on the alert for many years.

Each spring either the Omahas or Pawnees passed through the village on their way to visit some other tribe, and then returned in the fall. Then through the winter, stray bands would appear who had been hunting or fishing along the river.

As they were seen approaching, everything that could be was put under lock, and the doors of the houses were securely fastened. The Indians would wash and comb their hair at the water troughs, then gather everything about the yard that took their fancy. If by any chance they got into a house they would help themselves to eatables and if they could not find enough, they would demand more. They made a queer procession as they passed along the street. The bucks on the horses or ponies led the way, then would follow the pack ponies, with long poles fastened to each side and trailing along behind loaded with the baggage, then came the squaws, with their babies fastened to their backs, trudging along behind.

One early settler tells of her first experience with the Indians. She had just come from the far East, and was all alone in the house, when the door opened and three Indians entered, a buck and two squaws. They closed the door and placed their guns behind it, to show her that they would not harm her. They then went to the stove and seated themselves, making signs to her that they wanted more fire. She made a very hot fire in the cook stove.

The old fellow examined the stove until he found the oven door; this he opened and took three frozen fish from under his blanket and placed them upon the grate. While the fish were cooking, he made signs for something to eat. The lady said she only had bread and sorghum in the house. This she gave them, but the Indian was not satisfied; he made a fuss until she finally found that he wanted butter on his bread. She had to show him that the sorghum was all she had. They then took up the fish and went out of doors by the side of the house to eat it. After they were gone, she went out to see what they had left. She said they must have eaten every bit of the fish except the hard bone in the head, that was all that was left and that was picked clean.

Among the first settlers who came in 1855 was a young German who was an orphan and had had a hard life in America up to this time.

He took a claim and worked hard for a few years. He then went back to Quincy and persuaded a number of his own countrymen to come out to this new place and take claims, he helping them out, but they were to pay him back as they could.

Years passed; they each and all became very prosperous. But this first pioneer prospered perhaps to the greatest degree. The early settlers moved away one by one; as they left, he would buy their homes.

The houses were torn down or moved away, the trees and shrubs were uprooted, until now this one man, or his heirs—for he has gone to his reward—owns almost the whole of the once prosperous little village, and vast fields of grain have taken the place of the homes and streets.

It is hard to stand in the streets of the little village which now has about one hundred fifty inhabitants and believe that at one time it was the county-seat of Dodge county, and that it lacked only one vote of becoming the capital of the state. There are left only two or three of the first buildings. A short distance south of this village on a high bluff overlooking the river valley, and covered with oaks and evergreens, these early pioneers started a city which has grown for many years, and which will continue to grow for years to come. In this city of the dead we find many of the people who did much for the little village which failed, but who have taken up their abode in this beautiful spot, there to remain until the end of time.

This story of Fontenelle has been gathered from my early recollections of the place and what I have learned through grandparents, parents, and other relatives and friends.

My mother was raised in Fontenelle, coming there with her parents in 1856. She received her education in that first college.

My father was the son of one of the first Congregational missionaries to be sent there. I received my first schooling in the little village school.

Mrs. Eda Mead, in "Nebraska Pioneers," wrote the interesting story of the rise and fall of the Village of Fontanelle, Nebraska. These facts, as she avers, are largely from her own observation and memory, she having been reared in the vicinity herself. It is believed that no better account of this defunct village can be given at this time than the one .she gives, and from which we take the liberty to quote freely, that the story may be preserved in the annals of the county. (from Nebraska Genealogy, history of Fontanelle Township)[23]

---

[23]

https://nebraskagenealogy.com/washington/fontanelle_township_washington_county_nebraska.html

THE LAST ROMANTIC BUFFALO HUNT ON THE PLAINS OF NEBRASKA

BY JOHN LEE WEBSTER

In the autumn of 1872 a group of men, some of whom were then prominent in Nebraska history, Judge Elmer S. Dundy and Colonel Watson B. Smith, and one who afterward achieved national fame as an American explorer, Lieutenant Frederick Schwatka, and another who has since become known throughout Europe and America as a picturesque character and showman, Colonel Wm. F. Cody, participated in what proved to be the last romantic buffalo hunt upon the western plains of the state of Nebraska.

Elmer S. Dundy was a pioneer who had come to Nebraska in 1857. He had been a member of the territorial legislature for two successive terms; he was appointed a territorial judge in 1863 and became the first United States district judge after the admission of the state into the union. Colonel Watson B. Smith at that time held the office of clerk of the United States district and circuit courts for the district of Nebraska. Some years afterward he met a tragic death by being shot (accidentally or by assassination) in the corridors of the federal building in the city of Omaha. Colonel Smith was a lovable man, of the highest unimpeachable integrity and a most efficient public officer. There was also among the number James Neville, who at that time held the office of United States attorney and who afterward became a judge of the district court of Douglas county. He added zest, vim, and spirit by reason of some personal peculiarities to be mentioned later on.

These men, with the writer of this sketch, were anxious to have the experience and the enjoyment of the stimulating excitement of participating in a buffalo hunt before those native wild animals of the plains should become entirely extinct. To them it was to be a romantic incident in their lives and long to be remembered as an event of pioneer days. They enjoyed the luxury of a pullman car from Omaha to North Platte, which at that time was little more than a railway station at a division point upon the Union Pacific, and where was also located a military post occupied by a battalion of United States cavalry.

Lieutenant Frederick Schwatka, a regular army officer and American explorer, at one time commanded an arctic expedition in search of traces of the remains of Dr. Franklin. At another time he was in command of an exploring expedition of the Yukon river. At another time he commanded an expedition into the northernmost regions of Alaska in the interest of the New York *Times*. He also became a writer and the author of three quite well known books: *Along Alaska's Great River, Nimrod in the North,* and *Children of the Cold.*

At the time of which we are speaking Lieutenant Schwatka was stationed at the military post at North Platte. He furnished us with the necessary army horses and equipment for the hunting expedition, and he himself went along in command of a squad of cavalry which acted as an escort to protect us if need be when we should get into the frontier regions where the Indians were at times still engaged in the quest of game and sometimes in unfriendly raids.

William F. Cody, familiarly known as "Buffalo Bill," who had already achieved a reputation as a guide and hunter and who has since won a world reputation as a showman, went along with us as courier and chief hunter. He went on similar expeditions into the wilder regions of Wyoming with General Phil Sheridan, the Grand Duke Alexis, and others quite equally celebrated.

This Omaha group of amateur buffalo hunters, led by Buffalo Bill and escorted by Lieutenant Schwatka and his squad of cavalry, rode on the afternoon of the first day from North Platte to Fort McPherson and there camped for the night with the bare earth and a blanket for a bed and a small army tent for shelter and cover.

On the next morning after a rude army breakfast, eaten while we sat about upon the ground, and without the luxury of a bath or a change of wearing apparel, this cavalcade renewed its journey in a southwesterly direction expecting ultimately to reach the valley of the Republican. We consumed the entire day in traveling over what seemed almost a barren waste of undulating prairie, except where here and there it was broken by a higher upland and now and then crossed by a ravine and occasionally by a small stream of running water, along the banks of which might be found a small growth of timber. The visible area of the landscape was so great that it seemed boundless—an immense wilderness of space, and the altitude added to the invigorating and stimulating effect of the atmosphere.

We amateurs were constantly in anticipation of seeing either wild animals or Indians that might add to the spirit and zest of the expedition. There were no habitations, no fields, no farms. There was the vast expanse of plain in front of us ascending gradually westward toward the mountains with the blue sky and sunshine overhead. I do not recollect of seeing more than one little cabin or one little pioneer ranch during that whole day's ride. I do know that as the afternoon wore on those of us who were amateur horsemen were pleased to take our turns as the opportunity offered of riding in the army wagon which carried our supplies, and leading our horses.

When the shades of night of the second day had come we had seen many antelope and now and then heard the cry of the coyote and the wolf but we had not seen any sign of buffalo, but we did

222

receive information from some cattlemen or plain wanderers that there was a band of roving Indians in that vicinity which created in us a feeling of some anxiety—not so much for our personal safety as that our horses might be stolen and we be left in these remote regions without the necessary facilities for traveling homeward.

Our camp for the night was made upon a spot of low ground near the bank of a small creek which was bordered by hills on either side and sheltered by a small grove of timber near at hand. The surrounding hills would cut off the sight of the evening camp fires, and the timber would obscure the ascending columns of smoke as they spread into space through the branches of the trees.

The horses were picketed near the camp around the commissary wagon and Lieutenant Schwatka placed the cavalrymen upon sentinel duty. The night was spent with some restlessness and sleep was somewhat disturbed in anticipation of a possible danger, and I believe that all of us rather anxiously awaited the coming of the morning with the eastern sunlight that we might be restored to that feeling of security that would come with freedom of action and the opportunity for "preparedness." When morning did come, we had the pleasure of greeting each other with pleasant smiles and a feeling of happy contentment. We had not been molested by the Indians and our military sentinels had not seen them.

On the afternoon of the third day of our march into the wilderness we reached the farther margin of a high upland of the rim of a plain, where we had an opportunity of looking down over a large area of bottom land covered by vegetation and where there appeared to be signs of water. From this point of vantage, we discovered a small herd of browsing buffalo but so far away from us as to be beyond rifle range. These animals were apparently so far away from civilization or human habitation of any kind that their animal instinct gave them a feeling of safety and security.

We well knew that these animals could scent the approach of men and horses even when beyond the line of vision. We must study the currents of the air and plan our maneuvers with the utmost caution if we expected to be able to approach within any reasonable distance without being first discovered by them.

We entrusted ourselves to the guidance of Buffalo Bill, whose experience added to his good judgment, and so skillfully did he conduct our maneuvers around the hills and up and down ravines that within an hour we were within a reasonable distance of these wild animals before they discovered us, and then the chase began. It was a part of the plan that we should surround them, but we were prudently cautioned by Mr. Cody that a buffalo could run faster for a short distance than our horses. Therefore, we must keep far enough away so that if the buffalo should turn toward any of us, we could immediately turn and flee in the opposite direction as fast as our horses could carry us.

I must stop for a moment to recite a romantic incident which made this buffalo chase especially picturesque and amusing. Judge Neville had been in the habit of wearing in Omaha a high silk hat and a full dress coat (in common parlance a spiketail). He started out on this expedition wearing this suit of clothes and without any change of garments to wear on the hunt. So it came about that when this group of amateur buffalo huntsmen went riding pell-mell over the prairies after the buffalo, and likewise when pursued by them in turn, Judge Neville sat astride his running war-horse wearing his high silk hat and the long flaps of his spiketail coat floating out behind him on the breeze as if waving a farewell adieu to all his companions. He presented a picture against the horizon that does not have its parallel in all pioneer history.

It was entirely impossible for us inexperienced buffalo hunters while riding galloping horses across the plains to fire our rifles with any degree of accuracy. Suffice it to say we did not succeed in shooting any buffalo and I don't now even know that we tried to do so. We were too much taken up with the excitement of the chase and of being chased in turn. At one time we were the pursuers and at another time we were being pursued, but the excitement was so intense that there was no limit to our enjoyment or enthusiasm.

Buffalo Bill furnished us the unusual and soul-stirring amusement of that afternoon. He took it upon himself individually to lasso the largest bull buffalo of the herd while the rest of us did but little more than to direct the course of the flight of these wild animals, or perhaps, more correctly expressed—to keep out of their way. It did not take Buffalo Bill very long to lasso the large bull buffalo as his fleet blooded horse circled around the startled wild animal. When evening came, we left the lassoed buffalo out on the plains solitary and alone, lariated to a stake driven into the ground so firmly that we felt quite sure he could not escape. It is my impression that we captured a young buffalo out of the small herd, which we placed in a corral found in that vicinity.

On the following morning we went out upon the plains to get the lassoed buffalo and found that in his efforts to break away he had broken one of his legs. We were confronted with the question whether we should let the animal loose upon the prairies in his crippled condition or whether it would be a more merciful thing to shoot him and put him out of his pain and suffering. Buffalo Bill solved the vexatious problem by concluding to lead the crippled animal over to the ranchman's house and there he obtained such instruments as he could, including a butcher knife, a hand-saw, and a bar of iron. He amputated the limb of the buffalo above the point of the break in the bone and seared it over with a hot iron to close the artery and prevent the animal from bleeding to death. The surgical operation thus rudely performed upon this big, robust wild animal of the prairie seemed to be quite well and successfully performed. The buffalo was then left in the ranchman's corral with the understanding that he would see it was well fed and watered.

We were now quite a way from civilization and near the Colorado border line, and notwithstanding our subsequent riding over the hills and uplands during the following day we did not discover any other buffalo and those which had gotten away from us on the preceding day could not be found. During that day we turned northward, and I can remember that about noon we came to a cattleman's ranch where for the first time since our start on the journey we sat down to a wooden table in a log cabin for our noonday meal. During the afternoon we traveled northward as rapidly as our horses could carry us but night came on when we were twenty miles or more southwest of Fort McPherson and we found it again necessary to go into camp for the night, sleeping in the little army tents which we carried along with us in the commissary wagon.

Colonel Cody on this journey had been riding his own private horse—a beautiful animal, capable of great speed. I can remember quite well that Mr. Cody said that he never slept out at night when within twenty miles of his own home. He declined to go into camp with us but turned his horse to the northward and gave him the full rein and started off at a rapid gallop over the plains, expecting to reach his home before the hour of midnight. It seemed to us that it would be a desolate, dreary, lonesome and perilous ride over the solitude of that waste of country, without roads, without lights, without sign boards or guides, but Buffalo Bill said he knew the direction from the stars and that he would trust his good horse to safely carry him over depressions and ravines notwithstanding the darkness of the night. So, on he sped northward toward his home.

On the next day we amateur buffalo hunters rode on to Fort McPherson and thence to North Platte where we returned our army horses to the military post with a debt of gratitude to Lieutenant Schwatka, who at all times had been generous, courteous, and polite to us, as well as an interesting social companion.

So ended the last romantic and rather unsuccessful buffalo hunt over the western plains of the state of Nebraska—a region then desolate, arid, barren, and almost totally uninhabited, but today a wealthy and productive part of our state.

The story of the buffalo hunt in and of itself is not an incident of much importance but it furnishes the material for a most remarkable contrast of development within a period of a generation. The wild buffalo has gone. The aboriginal red man of the plains has disappeared. The white man with the new civilization has stepped into their places. It all seems to have been a part of Nature's great plan. Out of the desolation of the past there has come the new life with the new civilization, just as new worlds and their satellites have been created out of the dust of dead worlds.

There was a glory of the wilderness, but it has gone. There was a mystery that haunted all those barren plains but that too has gone. Now there are fields and houses and schools and groves of forest trees and villages and towns, all prosperous under the same warm sunshine as of a generation ago when the buffalo grazed on the meadow lands and the aboriginal Indians hunted over the plains.

JOHN LEE WEBSTER

Let me tell you something about the life and achievements of John Lee Webster, for whom Webster Street was named. The highlights of the Webster story, as reported in The Omaha World-Herald September 3, 1929 after Webster died at 82: "Since 1869, he had been one of Omaha's most vigorous and picturesque citizens, a leader at the bar, famed alike for his eloquence, his devotion to the arts, and his faith and pride in Omaha and Nebraska."

During his 60 years in residence in Nebraska after moving from Ohio, at age 22, Webster had quickly risen to prominence: President of the first state constitutional convention in 1875, attorney in many of the most important lawsuits fought in Omaha. Service as general counsel for the Metropolitan Utilities District and for the Omaha and Council Bluffs Street Railway Company. Webster headed the Nebraska delegation to the Republican National Convention in 1892. He served for six years as president of the Nebraska Historical Society. He was "famed for his lectures on Alexander Hamilton, and on the constitution," the World-Herald story said. He delivered lectures before

227

the state bar associations in Iowa, Colorado, Minnesota, and Nebraska. He called the United States Constitution "the greatest achievement of mankind."

Well known as a patron of the arts, Webster traveled to Europe frequently, bringing back works of art. He founded the Friends of Art Association in Nebraska. Until a few months before his death, Webster was still working as head of the committee, seeking to create a World War memorial in Omaha. The World-Herald account of his life noted that as an attorney Webster "had exceptional success," including famously his role in the historic trial which freed Ponca Chief Standing Bear from Army custody in Omaha and allowed him and his followers to return to their homeland along the Niobrara River rather than being forced to return to a reservation in what is now Oklahoma.

This, then, was the Webster for whom Webster Street was – and is – named: a prominent seven-block section.

Portrait and biographical sketch are available in "Omaha: The Gate City and Douglas County, Nebraska, A Record of Settlement, Organization of Settlement, Organization, Progress, and Achievement," Volume 2, 1917, pgs 986-989.

John married Josephine Watson on February 18, 1868 in Belle Vernon, PN. They had a daughter, Flora.[24]

---

[24] https://www.findagrave.com/memorial/73058561/john-lee-webster

We hope you have enjoyed what we believe to be the best kind of history book: firsthand accounts of our ancestors. It is our hope that you will make room in your home for a library filled with the true history books of America, and Western Civilization as a whole.

Knowledge Keepers is dedicated to the preservation of print materials to be passed on to future generations. Please visit our website for more history reprints, plus book lists and blog posts about the importance of preserving our history:

Knowledgekeepersbookstore.com

Please be so kind as to leave a review wherever you purchased this book!

Made in the USA
Middletown, DE
03 November 2023

41890373R00139